# CONSIDERING CHRISTIANITY:
How to Believe in a Secular Age

by Trevor Hamaker

Copyright 2020 by Trevor Hamaker

**ALL RIGHTS RESERVED.** No part of this publication may be reproduced or transmitted in any form without express written permission from the author.

Scripture quotations, unless otherwise noted, are taken from the Holy Bible, New Living Translation, copyright 1996, 2004, 2015 by Tyndale House Foundation. Used by permission of Tyndale House Publishers, Inc. Carol Stream, Illinois 60188. All rights reserved.

Scripture quotations marked NIV are from the Holy Bible, New International Version. Copyright 1973, 1978, 1984, 2011 by Biblica, Inc. Used by permission of Zondervan. All rights reserved worldwide. www.zondervan.com.

**ISBN-13:** 978-1-6947-8905-1

# Contents

Introduction: What's Going on Here? ..................................................1

Chapter 1: What Is Apologetics? ......................................................5

Chapter 2: Why Do We Believe What We Believe? ..........................11

Chapter 3: Why Won't Religion Go Away? ....................................21

Chapter 4: Why Doesn't Everyone Believe in God? .........................35

Chapter 5: What Are the Options? ................................................51

Interlude: Why Isn't God More Obvious? .........................................77

Chapter 6: Who Was Jesus? ............................................................83

Chapter 7: Are the Sources Reliable? ................................................99

Chapter 8: Where Do We Go from Here? ....................................111

About the Author ..........................................................................117

# INTRODUCTION
## What's Going on Here?

THE IDEA FOR this book formed when two of my worlds came together. I was a student in the Doctor of Ministry program at McAfee School Theology, and I was a teacher at a Christian high school. The high school's vision statement is, "Every student prepared to impact the world for Jesus Christ." But I had my suspicions that most of the students didn't feel as prepared as we hoped they would.

One day, I decided to ask them about it. I wrote the vision statement on the board in my classroom and said, "Who feels like this is true for you?" No hands went up. The room was very quiet. "Okay," I said, "what keeps you from feeling like this is true for you?" I was trying to understand the gap between where the students felt like they were and where the school aspired for them to be.

One by one, the students gave their answers. One student said, "I don't know how to talk about Christianity with other people." Another student said, "I can't answer my friends' questions about faith." Another said, "I'm having a hard time seeing how everything fits together." One more said, "I don't understand how believing in God actually makes a difference in *real* life." And then, after a few more students answered and the room felt safe, one student said, "I'm not sure I actually believe any of it."

Much to my surprise, they were all in their own way talking about apologetics. That was surprising because they had already read at least three different books on apologetics as part of the school's curriculum.

But something was obviously missing. I repeated the same exercise with all of my classes that day; the response was the same in every class.

I promised the students that I would try to help them. After all, that's what teachers are supposed to do, right? For the next few weeks, I thought about what they had told me that day in class. Then it hit me. The problem wasn't that they didn't know about Jesus. And the problem wasn't that they didn't know about apologetics. They knew plenty about both of those topics. The problem was that no one had helped them connect the dots and bring the scattered pieces of information together. No one had ever taken the time to build a case for Christianity from the ground up. Everything they had ever heard or read about Christianity started from a position of faith and assumed a posture of belief on their part. But that's an assumption we can't afford to make anymore.

Around that time, I was taking a class at McAfee School of Theology. One of the books that I was assigned to read for the class was *How (Not) to Be Secular* by James K. A. Smith. The book featured Smith's summaries of important insights from Charles Taylor's massive book, *A Secular Age*. It was enlightening, to say the least. I underlined sentence after sentence and put asterisks next to paragraphs on every page. Taylor, and Smith after him, had tapped into the cultural reasons behind what I was hearing from my students.

So, I went back to the drawing board. What would it look like if I didn't assume that my students believed anything about Jesus? How would I make a case for Christianity, given what I had learned about our secular age? I decided to start building the case from the ground up. I wanted to go piece by piece and show how it all fit together to form a coherent picture.

I announced to all my classes that I would be teaching a new unit on apologetics to address their questions. I told them to stop me at any time to ask questions or ask for clarifications. I invited them to share their thoughts at every point along the way. They responded with great enthusiasm. Day after day, we filled the whiteboard in my classroom with notes, ideas, and insights from the discussion that ensued around the material. It was a lively, exciting time.

We began by talking about the nature of apologetics and how belief actually works. We moved to a discussion about knowledge, namely, how do we know what we think we know? From there, we touched on potential reasons why religion has persisted in the world, despite sociologists' repeated suggestions that religion is going away.

We talked through the barriers to belief that they and their friends think about and talk about. We broke down, in detail, the only three options they have when it comes to the question of whether God exists. They wanted to know why God wasn't more obvious, so we talked about that.

Then we pivoted to a focused discussion about Jesus, what he said and did, how he died, and the resurrection. There's no doubt that Jesus is a compelling figure, but can we trust that the Gospels – Matthew, Mark, Luke, and John – told the story straight? Are they reliable sources? We covered that too. Through it all, the students were interested and engaged. They had moments when they were perplexed and moments when they felt the light bulbs turn on.

I thought about how to wrap up the unit. We had covered quite a bit of ground in a relatively short amount of time. The students had been stretched, and their faith had been strengthened. What was the best way to bring it all together? Religious violence was in the news, so I decided to talk about good and bad expressions of faith.

I wanted to publish this material because the way it affected my students was profound. Their responses were overwhelmingly positive, and many expressed gratitude that I had taken the time to explain these things in a way that they felt was both thorough and fair.

## Where Are We Going?

The chapters in this book follow the same order as the topics we discussed in my class. I've written in a conversational tone that scholars wouldn't be happy with, but that's okay. This book isn't for them. It's for ordinary people who are asking practical questions about faith. If you're considering Christianity or wondering how it's possible to keep believing in a secular age, then this book is for you.

The best way to enter into this material is to imagine that you and I are sitting together at your local coffee shop. We're catching up on everything that's going on, and then our conversation takes a spiritual turn. That's where this book starts. So, get a refill of your drink and let's continue the conversation.

# CHAPTER 1
# What Is Apologetics?

I'M CONCERNED THAT many Christians aren't confident about their faith. They've picked up on different pieces of Christianity through sermons, songs, blogs, and books, but they haven't been able to bring all of the pieces together in a satisfactory way. They hear about the stories of Scripture and the teachings of Jesus, and they want to believe them. But they're haunted by a question: Is this really true? Maybe that's your question too.

The present time has been described as a "secular age" by philosopher Charles Taylor.[1] According to Taylor, over a relatively short period of time, we've shifted "from a society where belief in God is unchallenged and indeed, unproblematic, to one in which it is understood to be one option among others, and frequently not the easiest to embrace."[2] Journalist Collin Hansen notes a similar shift, saying, "Faith is now more difficult than unbelief."[3] It seems Bob Dylan was onto something in 1964 when he sang, "The times they are a-changing."

What makes our situation so confusing today is that unbelief isn't automatic either. While many people find it difficult to believe in God, there are many other people who find it just as hard to *not* believe in God. It turns out that there are many thoughtful, well-intentioned

---

1 Charles Taylor, *A Secular Age* (Cambridge: The Belknap Press of Harvard University Press, 2007).
2 Ibid., 3.
3 Collin Hansen, "Hope In Our Secular Age," in *Our Secular Age: Ten Years of Reading and Applying Charles Taylor,* ed. Collin Hansen (Deerfield: The Gospel Coalition, 2017), 4.

people on both sides of questions about God. And there are doubters on both sides too. In fact, it could be said that doubt is the distinctive feature of our time. No one is immune to doubts about the existence of God, the meaning of life, and hope for the future. We feel we can be sure of very little and certain about even less. In our secular age, doubt visits both believers and non-believers alike.

Part of our doubt can be attributed to the overwhelming amount of information and choices that are available to us. It seems like we have an endless array of options when it comes to anything from restaurants to religions. As a result, those of us who profess faith, do so despite being "haunted by an inescapable sense of its contestability."[4] After all, we could be wrong.

How, in this secular age, can a person sort through the confusion and think clearly about faith? I think the answer comes from apologetics. The word "apologetics" is actually a bit misleading. It sounds like offering an apology. Indeed, that's what the word means. But to apologize for something has taken on a different connotation as time has passed. Today, to apologize for something means to acknowledge wrong-doing. In the past, however, to offer an apology meant to provide reasons for believing a particular thing or behaving a certain way. Apologetics, therefore, is simply about giving a reason (or reasons) for why you believe something, do something, or don't do something.

On the one hand, Christian apologetics tries to commend the faith to others. One the other hand, it tries to defend the faith against naysayers. Today, however, *we* must become the object of our own apologetic arguments. Our secular age makes us feel adrift. We are cross-pressured and fragilized. We sense the angst that comes from an over-emphasis of immanence at the expense of transcendence. Therefore, we have to commend and defend the truth of Christian faith to ourselves. In the words of Martin Lloyd Jones, "The main art in the matter of spiritual living is to know how to handle yourself. You have to take yourself in hand, you have to address yourself, preach

---

[4] James K. A. Smith, *How (Not) to Be Secular: Reading Charles Taylor* (Grand Rapids: Wm. B. Eerdmans, 2014), 4.

## Chapter 1: What Is Apologetics?

to yourself, question yourself."[5] Because belief is always contested, we have to reconsider the case and renew our commitment over and over again.

For some people, apologetics sounds like a head-trip, an intellectual detour away from what they see as an emotion-based topic. "After all," such a person might say, "God isn't interested in making sure we know all the answers to every possible question." And that person would be right. God's goal is higher than that. God wants us to trust him and love him, not merely know about him or be able to recite stock answers to slippery questions.

But what if your intellect and emotions, your head and your heart, aren't as far apart as some people make them seem? What if emphasizing emotions at the expense of intellect actually creates a false dichotomy, separating what was meant to be held together? What if the primary way to access your heart is through your head? That's exactly what philosophers Peter Kreeft and Ronald Tacelli insist happens. They say, "The head is important precisely because it is a gate to the heart. We can only love what we know."[6] Think about it, and I think you'll agree.

To illustrate what Kreeft and Tacelli mean, I can't do any better than to bring up my relationship with my wife. When I first met my wife, I was attracted to her, but I didn't love her; I didn't even know her. As we dated, I came to know her more. I discovered that I could trust her. Over time, I fell in love with her and committed my life to her. Do you see how the process worked? As my knowledge of her and trust in her grew, so did my love for her and commitment to her. That's also how it works in a person's relationship with God.

Knowledge about God and thinking about faith aren't ends in themselves. They're means to an end. Our knowledge about God is meant to inform our trust and support our commitment to God. That's why it's a false dichotomy to separate the head from the heart. We need both.

---

5 D. Martyn Lloyd-Jones, *Spiritual Depression: Its Causes and Its Cure* (Grand Rapids: Eerdmans, 1965), 21.
6 Peter Kreeft and Ronald Tacelli, *Handbook of Christian Apologetics* (Downers Grove: InterVarsity Press, 1994), 21.

But someone might protest that they've known people at church who know a lot about God but don't seem to love God (or other people) very much. That can happen, but it doesn't undermine what's being suggested here. We agree that knowing about someone isn't the same thing as loving them. You can know a lot about a person and not love them. That's possible. But what's being suggested here is that you can't love someone that you don't know. You can have knowledge without love, but you can't have love without knowledge.

## Two Sides of the Same Coin

The Apostle Paul addresses both sides of the knowledge-love coin. To the Corinthians, he says, "Knowledge puffs up while love builds up" (1 Corinthians 8:1 NIV). I usually hear this verse quoted by people who prefer a brand of faith that doesn't concern itself too much with theological precision. They say, "Just give me Jesus, not all of that confusing theological stuff." They roll their eyes when someone presses them on what they mean when they make statements about God and God's ways in the world.

Another favorite verse for these people, which they use as a catch-all for everything they don't want to think about, is Isaiah 55:9. In that verse, God says, "Just as the heavens are higher than the earth, so my ways are higher than your ways and my thoughts than your thoughts." With these two verses, the idea of spending time and energy thinking about faith is dismissed by these people as irrelevant at best and harmful at worst.

If these two verses were all the Bible had to say about the matter, then seeking knowledge to strengthen your faith would be a dangerous proposition. But these two verses don't tell the whole story. In Romans 10, the Apostle Paul suggests that it's a lack of knowledge about God and God's ways that has kept the Jewish people from recognizing Jesus as the Messiah and responding to him as they should. He says, "My heart's desire and prayer to God for the Israelites is that they may be saved. For I can testify about them that they are zealous for God, but their zeal is not based on knowledge" (Romans 10:1-2 NIV).

This is the counterpoint to the claim that knowledge puffs up. It's possible that for some people, knowledge will puff up, but that doesn't mean that the pursuit of knowledge for the sake of faith should be abandoned. Far from it. Zeal for God without proper knowledge of God is just as misguided. The risk we take when we abandon the pursuit of knowledge is that our faith will be mistaken, misdirected, and misapplied.

Dallas Willard, a philosophy professor at the University of Southern California, sought to clarify this connection between knowledge and commitment in Christian faith. He wrote, "Knowledge and commitment . . . are not exclusive of one another; rather, they are related. If we do not have knowledge of God at the foundation of our commitment, that commitment will simply not hold up."[7] Like a house with a weak foundation, faith without knowledge is bound to come crashing down. When it comes to faith, your head and your heart aren't at odds; they're intricately linked together.

## Why You Can't Just Believe

Kreeft and Tacelli also point out another reason why it's important to reflect on the intellectual aspects of faith. They say, "We can't believe what we believe to be untrue."[8] This makes sense when we consider an example: If you told me that you would give me $1 million if I believed that elephants could fly, I would try my hardest to believe it. But there would be one big problem: I don't believe it. In reality, I think that it's impossible for an elephant to fly. So, you would be off the hook. You wouldn't need to give me $1 million, much less even $1, because I can't force myself to believe what I believe can't happen.

Kenneth Daniels, a former missionary who eventually walked away from his Christian faith, understands how belief works. Why did he leave Christianity behind? He explains, "I found I had no choice but to believe what I thought to be true and to disbelieve what I thought to be untrue. . . . Admonitions like, 'You must choose to believe' are

---

7 Dallas Willard, *The Allure of Gentleness: Defending the Faith in the Manner of Jesus* (New York: HarperCollins, 2015), 81.
8 Kreeft and Tacelli, *Handbook of Christian Apologetics*, 21.

incomprehensible to me."[9] The fact is that a person can't believe what he or she thinks is ultimately illogical, impossible, or untrue. So, Daniels speaks for all of us when he concludes, "I believe what I believe *because I think it's true.*"[10]

This is why it doesn't do any good for a pastor to insist that you "just believe" the stories about Jesus or the teachings of Christianity. You *won't* just believe because you *can't* just believe. If you could, maybe you would. But you can't, even if we raise the stakes by saying that heaven and hell hang in the balance. Real belief simply doesn't work like that. We require real reasons to support and sustain what we really believe.

## What We Covered in This Chapter

In this chapter, I briefly described our secular age. It's a time in which we have a surplus of options and a staggering amount of doubt. Apologetics, or giving reasons for why we believe what we believe, is a helpful way to cut through the confusion. Some people push back against an intellectual approach to faith; they emphasize emotions instead. However, it's important to recognize that you can't have love without knowledge. Our heads are the pathway to our hearts. Ultimately, we believe what we believe because we think it's true.

But that final observation leads to an interesting question that we'll look at in the next chapter: Why do we believe some things are true and other things aren't?

---

9 Kenneth W. Daniels, *Why I Believed: Reflections of a Former Missionary* (Duncanville: Kenneth W. Daniels, 2009), 55.
10 Ibid.

# CHAPTER 2
# Why Do We Believe What We Believe?

SAMUEL SHENTON WAS a sign maker in England in the middle of the 20th century. But that's not what made him famous. Shenton's fame came from his belief that the earth is flat instead of round. He had elaborate models and detailed charts to explain his theory. He gave lectures and held meetings to advance his ideas. In 1956, he founded the Flat Earth Society to boost the credibility and reach of his cause. Later, when he was confronted with pictures of the earth that were taken from space, he dismissed them as fake. Samuel Shenton believed that the earth is flat, and no amount of evidence could convince him that it wasn't.[11]

Shenton's story brings the question of this chapter into focus: Why do we believe what we believe? Theologian John Stackhouse supplies an answer to this question that I think is exactly right. He says, "You cannot believe what you do not have adequate grounds – that is, what *to you* are adequate grounds – to believe."[12] To state it positively, you believe what you believe because you are convinced that you have good enough reasons to believe it. If you weren't convinced that you had sufficient grounds to believe something, you wouldn't believe it. It's that simple. But notice how Stackhouse has qualified his statement

---

11  Danny Lewis, "The Curious History of The International Flat Earth Society," Smithsonian.com (January 29, 2016). Online: https://www.smithsonianmag.com/smart-news/curious-history-international-flat-earth-society-180957969/
12  John G. Stackhouse, Jr., *Need to Know: Vocation as the Heart of Christian Epistemology* (New York: Oxford University Press, 2014), 208.

about adequate grounds with the words "to you." What you and I think counts as adequate grounds might not be the same thing. That's why two people might disagree about what is believable.

At this point, it's reasonable to ask if a person can believe something without adequate grounds. After all, many people believe things that seem to me to be unfounded. Does that undermine Stackhouse's claim? I think the answer is no, as long we keep Stackhouse's qualification intact: The grounds must be adequate to the individual doing the believing. We can test this by considering the case of Santa Claus.

Why do children believe in Santa? A few ideas come to mind: Their parents told them that Santa is real. Movies reinforce the claim that Santa is real. They sit on Santa's lap at stores in the weeks leading up to Christmas morning. Google provides a Santa Tracker that allows children to track Santa's movements around the globe on Christmas Eve. And finally, when a child wakes up on Christmas morning, the cookies are gone, and presents are under the tree. On their own or combined, these things provide what children perceive to be adequate grounds for believing in Santa.

But you don't believe in Santa, do you? Of course not. Neither do I. Somewhere along the way, you and I stopped seeing those factors listed above as constituting adequate grounds for belief. It occurred to us that our parents' claims, Christmas movies, Santa impersonators, Santa Trackers, and missing cookies were inadequate grounds for believing in Santa. Or maybe the whole charade stopped when your parents finally told you that Santa wasn't real. Either way, our adequate grounds for believing in Santa became inadequate. They were replaced by adequate grounds for disbelieving in Santa. That's when we stopped believing.

It might surprise you to learn that the same thing can happen when it comes to Christian faith. If you don't sense that you have adequate grounds to believe the claims of Christian faith, you won't believe. It's that simple. You believe something when you encounter what you perceive to be adequate grounds for that belief. That's how it works.

Chapter 2: Why Do We Believe What We Believe?

## How Do We Know What We Know?

The question of how we know things takes us into the subject of epistemology, a field of study within philosophy that addresses how we can know what we know. It's a complex subject that could be explored in far more detail than we'll do here, but it needs to be discussed at least briefly at this point.

In the fourth century BC, Master Chuang of China asked, "If when I am asleep I am a man dreaming I am a butterfly, how do I know when I am awake that I am not a butterfly dreaming I am a man?" This idea is common in Eastern conceptions of the world. The idea is that what you see is an illusion; it's not really real. Life, then, is like being stuck with Leonardo DiCaprio in the movie *Inception,* like a dream within a dream that only feels like it's real. Even as that movie ends, it's hard to tell if what you're seeing is the real world or another dream world.

Christian faith moves in a different direction. What you see is not an illusion, but reality. This is an outlook known as "realism," the belief that "we have reliable access to reality."[13] Christian philosopher Os Guinness explains, "in strong contrast to the Eastern views, the Christian view has a solid appreciation of the created reality that we know and that we may trust."[14] Even though Christians (and other realists) believe we have trustworthy access to reality, we must also recognize our limitations.

One limitation is that we're finite. As finite human beings, we are limited to bodies in specific times and places. We don't possess an all-seeing eye. We aren't capable of knowing everything there is to know. And even if we could know everything there is to know about a particular subject or problem, we would have no way of knowing that we did, in fact, know everything there is to know about that subject or problem. Therefore, John Stackhouse cautions, "we must beware of over-estimating the reliability of what we think we know."[15]

---

13 Stackhouse, *Need to Know,* 86.
14 Os Guiness, *Fool's Talk: Recovering the Art of Christian Persuasion* (Downers Grove: InterVarsity Press, 2015), 77.
15 Stackhouse, *Need to Know,* 87.

Another limitation is that we're fallen. According to Christian theology, our thoughts, perceptions, and choices have been disordered by sin. It's like sin creates a reality-distortion field that clouds our vision and skews our judgments. As a result, Stackhouse observes that "we are inclined in certain respects both to perceive things wrongly and to process what we perceive wrongly as well."[16] Because of these two factors – our finitude and our fallenness – we should include a healthy dose of skepticism about our realism. We have to practice a kind of "critical realism."

So, from the perspective of critical realism, how do we know what we know? The simplest way to answer that question is to say that we rely on authorities. An authority is someone or something that we rely on to describe or define reality for us. Whenever a person claims to know something, you can find out what serves as their authority for that knowledge by asking a single question: How do you know that? Whatever the person says in response to that question is serving as that person's authority. And if you disagree with the person's claim, it's usually because you attribute a lower level of trustworthiness to the authority they've cited. This also goes back to the earlier discussion about what constitutes "adequate grounds" to believe something.

## Four Sources of Knowledge

Generally speaking, we rely on four authoritative sources of knowledge. Though some philosophers might split them or consolidate them in different ways, the four main sources of our knowledge are experience, reason, community, and revelation. It will be helpful to explain a little bit about each one here.

### *Experience*

Experiences of seeing, hearing, tasting, smelling, and feeling help us figure out many things. As we grow up, we draw upon the memories created by our experiences to form generalizations and make decisions about the way the world works. Sometimes, however, we draw the

---
16 Ibid., 89.

wrong conclusions from our experiences because we haven't interpreted them properly, with reference to the other sources of knowledge.

Thomas Gilovich, a psychology professor at Cornell University, did research and wrote a book about drawing the wrong conclusions. According to Gilovich, our conclusions are questionable when they're based on incomplete pieces of information that don't represent the broader scope of the issue at hand.[17] Additionally, he points out that "we are inclined to adopt self-serving beliefs about ourselves, and comforting beliefs about the world."[18] In other words, our interpretations of our experiences aren't always accurate or trustworthy. Experience, therefore, while helpful, still needs to be balanced by the input that comes from the other sources of knowledge to be trusted.

## *Reason*

Reason involves "the orderly investigation of and reflection upon the world."[19] As such, reason helps us balance the subjectivity of our experiences with the objectivity of deliberation. When we employ reason, we aim to see a more complete picture than can be seen through the eyes of individual experience. We can learn things about reality when we pay attention, ask questions, form hypotheses, and draw conclusions. This process has been the driving force behind many of our most significant medical and technological advances. Philosophy professor Peter McInerney believes, "Careful and systematic perception can avoid almost all perceptual errors."[20] In other words, using reason to identify and interpret reality can eliminate most of the mistakes we make when we rely solely on our experience.

But we can't escape the fact that no matter how objective we try to be in our reasoning, we still aren't neutral. Researcher Ziva Kunda has documented how we come to the reasoning process with beliefs

---

17 Thomas Gilovich, *How We Know What Isn't So: The Fallibility of Human Reason in Everyday Life* (New York: The Free Press, 1991), 47-48.
18 Ibid., 78.
19 Stackhouse, *Need to Know*, 106.
20 Peter K. McInerney, *Introduction to Philosophy* (New York: HarperPerennial, 1992), 45.

and biases that shape what we see. Though we may attempt to be purely rational and maintain an "illusion of objectivity," we are susceptible to reading the evidence in a way that suits us.[21] In other words, sometimes we see what we want to see. So, while reason is an important and valuable source of knowledge, it must still be brought into conversation with input from the other sources.

## *Community*

We also learn from our community, by which I mean the people, traditions, and culture that surround us. "Much of what we believe about the world is not based on our own observations, but rather on what other people have told us."[22] This is how it has to be because no one can know everything about everything. When my car has an issue, I take it to the mechanic. When my body has an issue, I go see a doctor. The mechanic and the doctor share their knowledge with me about the problems. If I trust their authority (which, as I said above, is their ability to describe or define reality), then I'll act in accordance their suggestions. If I don't trust their authority, then I'll seek a second opinion about my issues.

Beyond that, it's clear that we rely on our community for a range of other things that we know. How do you know that the earth is round? Unless you're an astronaut, you're relying on the observations and trustworthiness of others for that information. How do you know that you were born on the date you now call your birthday? It's doubtful that you recall the event of your birth, so you're relying on the trustworthiness of your parents or the person who filled out your birth certificate for that information. When is Christmas? The answer depends on the community with which you identify. The church in the West celebrates Christmas on December 25 while the Eastern Orthodox Church celebrates it on January 7. The list could go on.

In all of these ways, our community serves as an authoritative source of knowledge for us. However, communities can (and often do)

---

21 Ziva Kunda, "The Case for Motivated Reasoning," *Psychological Bulletin* 108, number 3, (November 1990), 480-498.
22 McInerney, *Introduction to Philosophy*, 48.

pass along flawed versions of reality that should be called into question. For that reason, the knowledge we gain from our community must also be considered in light of the other sources of knowledge.

## Revelation

The last source of knowledge is revelation, though I recognize that revelation is not accepted as a source of knowledge by all people. Revelation is the label for knowledge that is revealed to us from beyond us. Such knowledge can come to a person through dreams, visions, voices, events, and many other mediums. In *Revelation and Reason,* Swiss theologian Emil Brunner explains, "Revelation always means that something hidden is made known, that a mystery is unveiled." He goes on, "Revelation means a supernatural kind of knowledge – given in a marvelous way – of something that man, of himself, could never know."[23]

Revelation is often thought to be a religious concept, but it also plays a role for many who aren't necessarily religious. People who do creative work, for example, often attribute their creativity to a muse. A muse is a personification of creative inspiration, but that doesn't take away from the fact that these people readily acknowledge that ideas have come to them from beyond them.

For a Christian, the Bible reveals truths that couldn't be known otherwise. For example, Genesis 1-2 tell us that God created us on purpose for a purpose. We could not discover that knowledge on our own. First John 4:8 tells us that God is love. Again, we wouldn't know that if it weren't revealed to us. That's why Eugene Peterson suggests that reading the Bible "takes us off guard, surprises us, and draws us into its reality."[24] As the Bible unveils its insights about reality, it "pulls us into participation with God on *his* terms" rather than our own.[25]

---

23 Emil Brunner, *Revelation and Reason: The Christian Doctrine of Faith and Knowledge* (Philadelphia: The Westminster Press, 1946), 23.
24 Eugene H. Peterson, *Eat This Book: A Conversation in the Art of Spiritual Reading* (Grand Rapids: Wm. B. Eerdmans, 2006), 6.
25 Ibid.

Even so, the Bible doesn't say anything about many of the topics and issues that affect us today. Theologian Roger Olson acknowledges, "Abortion is almost absent from the Bible. Nothing [in the Bible] speaks directly to cremation. The thorny problems of modern economics find few if any solutions in the Bible. And what about cloning? It wasn't even envisioned by the biblical authors."[26] All of this means that revealed knowledge can't be used in isolation. It needs to be considered in light of what we learn from the other sources of knowledge.

## Bringing It All Together

These four sources of knowledge don't form a hierarchy; they don't compete against one another. They're complementary of each other. Or, as Dallas Willard explains, they "are not inherently opposed, but are well-suited to supplement each other in the course of real life."[27] Legend tells us that King Arthur set up a round table for meetings with his knights. Because the table was round, there wasn't a head position, and decisions could be made without reference to any individual's hierarchy or status. The sources of knowledge could be pictured to function in the same way as King Arthur's round table. Experience, reason, community, and revelation each get a seat, and all of them get a chance to speak.

An over-reliance on experience might cause a person to form mistaken generalizations and prejudices about other people. That's what Malcolm Gladwell found when he investigated the issue of racism. Gladwell concluded that racism is often connected to our first impressions, which are "generated by our experiences and our environment."[28] But Gladwell knows that our experiences can be unreliable guides to reality, so he suggests we take "active steps to manage and

---

26 Roger E. Olson, *Questions to All Your Answers: A Journey from Folk Religion to Examined Faith* (Grand Rapids: Zondervan, 2007), 87.
27 Dallas Willard, *Knowing Christ Today: Why We Can Trust Spiritual Knowledge* (New York: HarperOne, 2009), 60.
28 Malcolm Gladwell, *Blink: The Power of Thinking Without Thinking* (New York: Little, Brown and Company, 2005), 97.

control those impressions."[29] We manage and control our impressions by supplementing our experiences with other sources of knowledge.

Likewise, if a person relies on revelation alone, without consulting other sources of knowledge, he might do something harmful. Consider, for example, the case of Hemy Neuman. Neuman was in love with his employee, Andrea Sneiderman. But she was married. So, one morning, when Andrea Sneiderman's husband was dropping off their kids at daycare, Neuman shot and killed him in the parking lot. During his court trial, Neuman appealed to revelation, saying that an angel visited him and told him to kill Andrea's husband.[30] Factoring in the insights of reason and community could have prevented that tragedy.

Understanding the sources of knowledge as complementary rather than hierarchical can also take us passed many of the futile debates between science and religion. John Stackhouse notes, "There is no actual conflict between *any* science and Christianity."[31] That's because they're both authoritative sources of knowledge, and they function in a complementary way, not a hierarchical way. For example, the Bible doesn't provide a cure for cancer; we need science for that. And science doesn't tell us what God is like or what life is for; we need the Bible for that.

Christians should welcome all truth that coheres with and corresponds to reality no matter where it comes from. Or, as the early Christian theologian Augustine said, "Let every good and true Christian understand that wherever truth may be found, it belongs to his Master."[32] In short, all truth is God's truth.

---

29 Ibid., 98.
30 Ashley Bridges and Alice Gomstyn, "Dunwoody Sentencing: Hemy Neuman Gets Life in Prison, No Parole," *ABC News*, March 15, 2012, https://abcnews.go.com/US/dunwoody-verdict-hemy-neuman-found-guilty/story?id=15928911.
31 Stackhouse, *Need to Know*, 107.
32 St. Augustine and J. F. Shaw, *On Christian Doctrine* (Mineola: Dover Publications, 2009), 53.

## What We Covered in This Chapter

In this chapter, we moved the conversation forward by discussing why we believe what we believe and how we know what we know. According to Christianity, the world isn't an illusion; we have reliable access to reality. However, we are also finite and fallen creatures. What we see and think can sometimes be skewed and off-base. This approach to the world is called critical realism. Generally speaking, we are informed by experience, reason, community, and revelation. These sources can be called authoritative insofar as we trust them to describe or define reality for us. They're meant to be complementary rather than hierarchical. Ultimately, we should welcome the truth from wherever it comes.

In the next chapter, we'll talk about an interesting phenomenon. Even though people have predicted the downfall of religion for over a hundred years, it's still not going away. Why not? That's the topic of the next chapter.

# CHAPTER 3
# Why Won't Religion Go Away?

According to Secularization Theory, "social and intellectual progress is rendering religion obsolete."[33] As the thinking goes, religion becomes increasingly marginalized as a society becomes increasingly modernized. Eventually, such a society will no longer rely upon religion at all. It should be noted that in this instance, religion is understood generically to mean "a belief that there is a reality beyond the reality of our ordinary experience, and that this reality is of great significance for human life."[34] It's that belief, the belief that there's more to this life than this life, that faces a questionable future. Or so we're told.

Friedrich Nietzsche wasn't the first to articulate the theory of secularization, but he was on the same track in 1882. That was the year he proclaimed, "God is dead." With that phrase, he claimed that the rationalism of the Enlightenment had eliminated the possibility of believing in God anymore. In other words, we don't need God anymore for anything.

## What Happens When We Imagine?

John Lennon, the musician who became famous with the Beatles, channeled his inner-Nietzsche in an interview in 1966. He said, "Christianity will go. It will vanish and shrink. I needn't argue about

---

33 William Sims Bainbridge, "Atheism," in *The Oxford Handbook of the Sociology of Religion,* ed. Peter B. Clarke (New York: Oxford University Press, 2009), 327.
34 Peter L. Berger, *The Many Altars of Modernity: Toward a Paradigm for Religion in a Pluralist Age* (Boston: De Gruyter, 2014), 17.

that; I'm right and I will be proved right."[35] Five years later, in 1971, he wrote the lyrics to "Imagine," a song in which he envisioned the end of all religions:

*"Imagine there's no heaven. It's easy if you try.*
*No hell below us. Above us only sky.*
*Imagine all the people, living for today."*

His lyrics make sense. If there's no afterlife after this life, then the only option is to live as if today is all you have. In that situation, today *is* all you have. But what if the thing someone wants to do while he "lives for today" is thought by others to be reckless or even evil? It doesn't really matter. There's no God to reward or punish anyone for anything, so you can do whatever you want. If it feels good, you should do it. Or, in Lennon's words, you should "live for today."

The song goes on:

*"Imagine there's no countries. It isn't hard to do.*
*Nothing to kill or die for. And no religion, too.*
*Imagine all the people, living life in peace."*

Here, Lennon puts his cards on the table. Religious beliefs work against peace. If people would just give up their religion, then everyone could live happily ever after. In Lennon's imagined, religion-less world, there's nothing to stand up against and nothing to give your life for.

But it was precisely the opposite vision that drove Martin Luther King, Jr. to lead the Civil Rights Movement just a few years before Lennon wrote these lyrics. King said, "If a man has not discovered something that he will die for, he isn't fit to live." It was King's religion that gave him the vision, energy, hope, and moral courage to work for peace rather than simply imagining it.

In the next lines of the song, Lennon the songwriter becomes Lennon the evangelist:

*"You may say that I'm a dreamer. But I'm not the only one.*
*I hope someday you'll join us. And the world will live as one."*

---

35 Maureen Cleave, "How Does a Beatle Live? John Lennon Lives Like This," in *London Evening Standard*, March 4, 1966.

Lennon believed that when religion was gone, along with the promise of heaven and the threat of hell, the new era would see an outpouring of love for people. But there's no evidence to support that belief. Commenting about violence in the twentieth century, Alister McGrath says, "Never before in human history had so many people been massacred in the name of so many secular ideologies, metanarratives, and visions of progress."[36] Contrary to Lennon's claims, it turns out that abandoning religion doesn't create more love for people; it creates more lust for power.

## A Matter of Preference

In a world without a higher sense of accountability, why should anyone help or support anyone else? If there's nothing more to this life than this life, then why should anyone put anyone else's needs above his own? Why *shouldn't* someone use and abuse others to get ahead and get his own way? To what moral authority can someone appeal to claim that love for people is better than lust for power? There isn't one. On what grounds can tolerance be said to be a higher virtue than intolerance? There aren't any.

The direction a person chooses, then, is left up to his or her own sense of personal preferences and opinions. The question of who or what is right is made unintelligible, like asking whether chocolate or vanilla ice cream is right. The answer is obviously neither. It's a matter of preference. And preferences can't be wrong. Nietzsche acknowledged this, saying, "Judgments, value judgments, concerning life, for or against, can in the last resort never be true."[37]

The call to abandon religion imagines a world filled with love for people, but, because it cuts itself off from the religious value system that produces love, it can only create a world filled with the lust for power. Again, Nietzsche saw this clearly. He says, "When one gives up Christian belief one thereby deprives oneself of the *right* to Christian

---

36 Alister McGrath, *Why God Won't Go Away: Is the New Atheism Running on Empty?* (Nashville: Thomas Nelson, 2010), 71-72.
37 Friedrich Nietzsche, *Twilight of the Idols and the Anti-Christ,* trans. R. J. Hollingdale (New York: Penguin Classics, 1990), 40.

morality. For the latter is absolutely *not* self-evident: one must make this point clear again and again in spite of English shallowpates."[38] A shallowpate is someone whose thinking is superficial and shallow, like an ignorant fool.

Nietzsche's point was this: Christian behaviors (like love, humility, generosity, and sacrifice) are intrinsically connected to Christian beliefs. Those beliefs lead to those behaviors. If you dismiss Christian beliefs, then you shouldn't expect people to exhibit Christian behaviors. That makes perfect sense, but Lennon doesn't seem to have grasped Nietzsche's point.

If Lennon's lyrics had stayed in the past, then I wouldn't need to bring them up here. But they didn't. In 2004 and 2010, "Imagine" was ranked by *Rolling Stone* as the third best song of all time. Since 2005, the song has been sung by music artists every year on New Year's Eve as the ball drops in Times Square. It was even used during the end credits of the Summer 2012 Olympics. Clearly, plenty of people still imagine a world in which religion has gone away. But their dream isn't coming true.

## Religion Isn't Going Away

Peter Berger, a sociologist and early proponent of the Secularization Theory, admits, "It took me quite a few years to reach the conclusion that secularization theory was empirically untenable."[39] Religion hasn't gone away in the (post)modern period; it has flourished. Berger explains, "On the cusp of the twentieth century, [Nietzsche] evoked a vision of empty, deserted altars. This is not what in fact occurred. Instead, the last century saw an enormous proliferation of altars. The proliferation continues."[40]

Jack Goldstone, professor of Public Policy at George Mason University, echoes Berger's assessment: "Sociologists jumped the gun when they said the growth of modernization would bring a growth of

---
38 Ibid., 80.
39 Berger, *The Many Altars of Modernity*, 19.
40 Ibid., 15.

secularization and unbelief. That is not what we are seeing. People want and need religion."[41] Religion isn't going away; it's here to stay.

Goldstone's last sentence – that people want and need religion – is interesting. Even though our wanting or needing something to be true doesn't mean that it *is* true, our wants and needs are something to think about. In his book, *Mere Christianity*, C. S. Lewis made the case that our desires attest to the possibility of their fulfillment. He wrote, "Creatures are not born with desires unless satisfaction for those desires exists."[42] For example, a hungry baby wants food because there's such a thing as food. That's not to say that every hungry baby will be fed. We know better than that, and so did Lewis. He conceded that it's possible for a starving man to die on a raft in the ocean. "But," he went on, "a man's hunger does prove that he comes from a race that repairs its body by eating and inhabits a world where eatable substances exist."[43]

So, if we find that people want and need religion, it might point to the existence of God as the one who can satisfy that desire. It's along these lines that Lewis offers his now-famous remark: "If I find in myself a desire which no experience in this world can satisfy, the most probable explanation is that I was made for another world."[44]

## Two Reasons Why Religion Won't Go Away

I see two primary reasons why religion won't go away: scientific shortcomings and experiences of transcendence. Let's take each one in turn.

---

41 Sarah Pulliam Bailey, "The World Is Expected to Become More Religious – Not Less," *Washington Post*, April 24, 2015. Online: https://www.washingtonpost.com/news/acts-of-faith/wp/2015/04/24/the-world-is-expected-to-become-more-religious-not-less/?utm_term=.47f9ed5eeeed
42 C. S. Lewis, *Mere Christianity* (New York: Touchstone, 1996), 121.
43 C. S. Lewis, *The Weight of Glory* (San Francisco: HarperOne, 1980), 31.
44 Lewis, *Mere Christianity*, 121.

## Scientific Shortcomings

By definition, science "deals only with the natural, the repeatable, that which is governed by law."[45] How, then, does science explain our existence? Prominent chemist and atheist Peter Atkins claims that the universe produced itself. He writes, "Spacetime generates its own dust in the process of its own self-assembly."[46] His argument that the universe perfectly assembled itself by itself to be a hospitable place for the production of life reminds me of the Infinite Monkey Theorem.

The Infinite Monkey Theorem says that a monkey hitting random keys on a computer keyboard for an infinite amount of time will eventually end up writing a complete work of Shakespeare. Surely, such an occurrence would be *possible*. But is it *probable?* An experiment conducted by students from the University of Plymouth intended to find out. The students left a computer in a cage with six monkeys at the Paignton Zoo in England to see what the monkeys would type with it. One of the monkeys hit the keyboard repeatedly with a rock. Other monkeys used the computer as a toilet. After a month, the monkeys had produced five pages, mostly filled with the letter S. They didn't type a single word of the English language.[47] Israeli scientist Gerald Schroeder calculated the probability of those monkeys typing a fourteen-line Shakespearean sonnet and found that the probability was 10 to the 690$^{th}$ power.[48] Atkins' proposal about creation assembling itself has an even lower probability than that.

Antony Flew spent sixty years as an atheist, becoming one of its premier academic advocates along the way. But there came a day when he could no longer deny what the evidence was leading him to conclude. He explains, "After more than six decades of atheism, I announced that I had changed teams, so to speak."[49] His new team

---
45 Michael Ruse, *Darwinism Defended* (Reading: Addison-Wiley, 1982), 322.
46 Peter W. Atkins, *Creation Revisited: The Origin of Space, Time and the Universe* (Harmondsworth, England: Penguin Science, 1994), 143.
47 Wikipedia Contributors, "Infinite monkey theorem," *Wikipedia, The Free Encyclopedia*, https://en.wikipedia.org/wiki/Infinite_monkey_theorem.
48 Antony Flew, *There Is a God: How the World's Most Notorious Atheist Changed His Mind* (New York: HarperOne, 2007), 76.
49 Ibid., 65.

acknowledged that the universe has a divine designer. Flew saw an intelligence behind creation, especially when he considered DNA. DNA research has shown the "almost unbelievable complexity of the arrangements which are needed to produce life," and, Flew concludes, "intelligence must have been involved in getting these extraordinarily diverse elements to work together."[50]

Another angle to consider is the question of where the raw material for the universe came from in the first place. Even if we grant what most scientists currently propose, that there was a big bang that brought our current cosmos into existence, it's reasonable to ask: What caused the bang?

As I understand it, the Law of Conservation of Mass states that matter can neither be created nor destroyed. So, has matter always existed? Is matter eternal, without beginning or ending? If someone answers yes, then they have stepped away from the realm of science because there is no way a person could test or know that apart from faith. It can't be proven scientifically. Maybe that's why at least one scientific textbook emphasizes that "science rests on faith."[51] It takes faith to believe in an eternal God, but it also takes faith to believe in eternal matter. The fact is, science "can prove neither the claim that there is a supernatural, transcendent reality nor the claim that there is none."[52] Proving such a thing is beyond the scope of science.

Finally, science also falls short in its ability to help us think about the things that matter most. Humans wrestle with questions that go beyond the scientific method. There are questions that science can't answer, such as "What are we all here for?" and "What's the point of living?"[53] Beyond that, Richard Dawkins, one of the leaders of the New Atheist movement, admits, "Science has no methods for deciding

---

50 Ibid., 75.
51 Hugh G. Gouch, *Scientific Method in Practice* (New York: Cambridge University Press, 2003), 152.
52 Timothy Keller, *Making Sense of God: An Invitation to the Skeptical* (New York: Viking, 2016), 53.
53 Peter B. Medawar, *The Limits of Science* (New York: Oxford University Press, 1988), 66.

what is ethical."[54] Even Albert Einstein acknowledged, "The content of scientific theory itself offers no moral foundation for the personal conduct of life."[55] It's not that scientists or scientifically-minded people can't wonder about morality or the meaning of life. They can and often do. But science itself isn't designed to inform them about those matters.

These are questions that troubled Paul Kalanithi, a neurosurgeon who died of cancer before he reached his fortieth birthday. Raised as a Christian, Kalanithi left his faith behind in college to become an atheist. "There is no proof of God," he reasoned, "therefore, it is unreasonable to *believe* in God."[56] But science has its shortcomings. Reflecting on life as he approached death, Kalanithi saw the situation differently. He writes, "Science may provide the most useful way to organize empirical, reproducible data, but its power to do so is predicated on its inability to grasp the most central aspects of human life: hope, fear, love, hate, beauty, envy, honor, weakness, striving, suffering, and virtue."[57] In other words, science can account for a lot of things, but it can't account for everything. Specifically, science can't account for the things that make us truly human. Kalanithi discovered that "scientific knowledge" is "inapplicable" to those things.[58] Before his death, he was drawn back to belief in God, compelled by the core values of Christian faith.[59]

## Experiences of Transcendence

In 1901 and 1902, psychologist William James delivered the esteemed Gifford Lectures at the University of Edinburgh in Scotland. His lectures were subsequently edited and published as *The Varieties of Religious Experience*. Among his comments, James pointed out that

---

54 Richard Dawkins, *A Devil's Chaplain: Reflections on Hope, Lies, Science, and Love* (New York: Mariner Books, 2004), 34.
55 Albert Einstein, James Murphy, and J.W.N. Sullivan, "Science and God: A German Dialogue," *The Forum*, June 1930, 374. Online: http://www.unz.com/print/Forum-1930jun-00373/
56 Paul Kalanithi, *When Breath Becomes Air* (New York: Random House, 2016), 168.
57 Ibid., 170.
58 Ibid.
59 Ibid., 171.

## Chapter 3: Why Won't Religion Go Away?

a scientific, rationalistic perspective can't explain everything about a person's thoughts or experiences. More directly, he said, "we have to confess that the part of [us] for which rationalism can give an account is relatively superficial."[60]

To back up his claim, James mentions times of discovery when our minds sense more going on than we initially perceived. "Single words, and conjunctions of words, effects of light on land and sea, odors and musical sounds, all bring [that sense] when the mind is turned right."[61] He talks about "dreamy states," which carry "a sense of mystery" and give us "the feeling of an enlargement of perception which seems imminent but never completes itself."[62] He cites the experience of 19th-century writer Charles Kingsley who described walking in the fields and becoming overwhelmed and awestruck with the feeling that everything has a significant yet inexplicable meaning. Kingsley's experience, according to James, is more common than we might think.[63] Throughout the book, James provides ample support to back up his claim. The lesson is that we should recognize that there's more going on in us and around us than first meets the eye.

Before the Enlightenment, the world had a sense of enchantment. The universe was open, and humanity was vulnerable to meaning and powers outside of our control. Since the Enlightenment, however, our enchanted world has become increasingly disenchanted. The universe feels closed, and humanity is increasingly cut off from meaning and powers outside of our control. James K. A. Smith describes our situation: "Diseases are not demonic, mental illness is no longer possession, the body is no longer ensouled."[64] In this situation, our problem isn't sin; that idea has been left behind. Our problem is sickness, which can be managed and treated. So, in our secular age, therapists have become the new pastors, and immanent concerns have replaced transcendent ones as our primary focus.

---

60 William James, *Varieties of Religious Experience* (New York: Longmans, Green, and Company, 1903), 73.
61 Ibid., 383.
62 Ibid., 384.
63 Ibid., 384-385.
64 Smith, *How (Not) to Be Secular*, 28.

But the disenchantment hasn't fully taken over yet. We still have experiences of transcendence in which we're haunted by the sense that this life isn't all there is. We can't escape the idea that there might be more to this life than this life. We still wonder if maybe there's something bigger than us, beyond us. We ask if it's possible that we were made for more than here and now? And we're struck by the thought that perhaps the world might actually be enchanted after all.

When Steve Jobs chose Walter Isaacson to write his biography, Isaacson was given unprecedented access to the Apple founder's life. As Jobs faced his impending death from pancreatic cancer, he told Isaacson, "For most of my life, I've felt that there must be more to our existence than meets the eye."[65] Though he wasn't sure about the existence of God, Jobs acknowledged how strange it would be if no part of us continues on after we die. "I like to think that something survives after you die. It's strange to think that you accumulated all this experience, and maybe a little wisdom, and it just goes away. So I really want to believe that something survives, that maybe your consciousness endures."[66] For Jobs, it makes sense that there would be more to this life than only this life. For others, the sense is less logical and more ethereal.

When writer Barbara Ehrenreich was seventeen, she woke up early one morning and took a walk as the sun rose. Walking in no particular direction, with no specific intention, she suddenly felt more than she'd felt before. She saw more than she'd seen before. "The world flamed into life," she remembers. "There were no visions, no prophetic voices or visits by totemic animals, just this blazing everywhere. Something poured into me and I into it. . . . It was a furious encounter with a living substance that was coming at me through all things at once."[67]

Transcendent reality had broken through her immanent frame. And even though she doesn't make the connection, Ehrenreich's experience is similar to biblical accounts of God's presence portrayed

---

65 Walter Isaacson, *Steve Jobs* (New York: Simon & Schuster, 2011), 571.
66 Ibid.
67 Barbara Ehrenreich, *Living with a Wild God: A Nonbeliever's Search for the Truth about Everything* (New York: Twelve Books, 2014), 115-116.

as fire and light. In Exodus 3:2, God appears to Moses as flames of fire from within a bush. In Deuteronomy 4:24, God is called a consuming fire. And in the vision of Revelation 21:23, the heavenly city doesn't need the sun to give it light because it's illuminated by the light of God's own glory.

Vaclav Havel was a Czechoslovakian political dissident who later became the first president of the Czech Republic. His actions as an activist resulted in multiple stays in prison. During his longest stint in prison, which lasted nearly four years, he was allowed to write letters to his wife, Olga. In one of his letters, he described being "overcome by a sensation that is difficult to describe." He was watching the leaves of a large tree against the backdrop of a clear sky, when, he felt like he was at the very "edge of the infinite." He says, "I was flooded with a sense of ultimate happiness and harmony with the world and with myself, with that moment, with all the moments I could call up, and with everything invisible that lies behind it and has meaning."[68] As he sat there, Havel experienced a re-enchantment of the world. He couldn't escape the sense of transcendence.

These experiences of transcendence point to what Marcus Borg calls "thin places," borrowing the term from early Celtic Christianity. Reality, according to Borg, has two layers or dimensions: visible and invisible. Thin places are where the two dimensions of reality overlap. They "are the places where the boundary between the two levels becomes very soft, porous, and permeable. Thin places are places where the veil momentarily lifts."[69] People often experience the veil being lifted through the arts, nature, and relationships. A case can even be made that one of the primary functions of Christian worship is to create a thin place for people to encounter God. However it happens, and whatever we call it, there continue to be moments when a person "experiences a fullness in which the world suddenly seems charged with meaning, coherence, and beauty that break in through our ordinary senses of being in the world."[70]

---

[68] Vaclav Havel, *Letters to Olga* (New York: Knopf, 1988), 331-332.
[69] Marcus Borg, *The Heart of Christianity: Rediscovering a Life of Faith* (New York: HarperCollins, 2004), 155-156.
[70] Keller, *Making Sense of God*, 18.

## The Parable of the Hidden Springs

Theologian N. T. Wright tells this parable to describe our culture's tenuous relationship with religion and spirituality.[71] A powerful dictator noticed that the many springs throughout the cities and towns that functioned as his country's water sources were often uncontrollable and sometimes dangerous. They could be beneficial for some people, but they could also become polluted or cause flooding. The dictator did what he thought was rational; he paved over all the springs and set up a system of water pipes that he could control. People got used to the new, efficient system and praised the dictator for being so practical.

A generation passed before, suddenly, the water beneath the concrete burst through, unable to be contained any longer. Wright explains, "We in the Western world are the citizens of that country. The dictator is the philosophy that has shaped our world for the past two or more centuries. . . . And the water is what we today call 'spirituality,' the hidden spring that bubbles up within human hearts and human societies."[72]

## What We Covered in This Chapter

In this chapter, I introduced the claim of Secularization Theory. For decades, sociologists predicted that the rise of modernity spelled the end of religion. But that didn't happen. Contrary to what John Lennon imagined, when societies adopt religion-less policies and practices, the result isn't love for people; the result is lust for power. And despite repeated calls from many people to do away with religion altogether, we find that we just can't take that step. While scientists do valuable work, the questions they're answering aren't always the questions we're asking. Science just isn't designed to do that kind of work. Therefore, we recognize scientific shortcomings. Additionally, we can't dismiss our desires for and experiences of transcendence. We can't shake the sense that perhaps there's more going on around us than meets the eye. And

---
71 N. T. Wright, *Simply Christian: Why Christianity Makes Sense* (New York: HarperOne, 2006), 17-18.
72 Ibid., 18.

we wonder if maybe we were made for more than right here and right now.

Given all of that, some people still don't believe in God. They encounter barriers to belief, and those barriers deserve to be addressed. That's the task of the next chapter.

# CHAPTER 4
# Why Doesn't Everyone Believe in God?

I DON'T WANT to give the impression that believing in God in general or Christianity in particular is an easy or automatic conclusion for thoughtful people to make. It's not. William J. O'Malley, a Catholic priest and teacher, admitted, "Anyone with a reasonably sophisticated education faces genuine obstacles to accepting an all-powerful, all-knowing, all-competent Entity whom no one has ever seen."[73]

The truth is, there are multiple factors that go into a person's conclusion about these matters. And some of those factors carry more weight than others for different people. Timothy Keller was a pastor for almost thirty years in New York City. In those years, he spent lots of time in conversations with religious seekers and skeptics. What he found was that "every person embraces his or her worldview for a variety of rational, emotional, cultural, and social factors."[74]

So, it's not as simple as saying that irreligious people are acting irrationally while religious people are acting rationally. Human beings don't operate within nicely compartmentalized schemes like that. Religious people are religious because of a combination of reasons. Likewise, irreligious people are irreligious because of a combination of reasons. In this chapter, then, I want to explore some of those reasons

---
73 William J. O'Malley, *God: The Oldest Question* (Chicago: Loyola Press, 2000), 4.
74 Keller, *Making Sense of God*, 4.

for unbelief – or, what could be called barriers to belief – and offer some responses that might be helpful to think about.

## Barrier #1: Believing in spiritual beings and forces is primitive, isn't it?

This barrier arose in the wake of the Enlightenment's claim that scientific progress would be the "light of the world," bringing salvation through knowledge, peace, and wealth to the ends of the earth. The claim has a tinge of cultural snobbery to it: "People who believe in God are living in the dark ages. They need to be enlightened. We used to believe in those outdated superstitions, but we know better than that now."

Part of the Enlightenment's approach was to rely on scientific naturalism, examining only natural causes and effects and leaving no room for God or spiritual forces to make a difference in the physical world. Philosopher William Hasker explains, "According to naturalism, everything which exists or occurs lies entirely within the domain of natural processes. Nothing comes into nature or influences it from outside."[75]

It's important to recognize that naturalism isn't neutral in its approach; it has an anti-supernatural bias. Francis Collins, director of the National Institutes of Health, explains that for someone who sees the world this way, "even an extremely unusual cure of cancer will be discounted as evidence of the miraculous, and will instead be chalked up to the fact that rare events will occasionally occur within the natural world."[76]

Naturalistic thinking became so pervasive that one Christian theologian acknowledged, "It is as impossible for most of us to believe in the real existence of demonic or angelic powers as it is to believe

---

75 William Hasker, *Metaphysics: Constructing a World View* (Downers Grove: InterVarsity Press, 1983), 108.
76 Francis S. Collins, *The Language of God: A Scientist Presents the Evidence for Belief* (New York: Free Press, 2006), 50-51.

in dragons, elves, or a flat world."[77] But why should that be the case? Has science somehow disproved the existence of spiritual beings in a spiritual dimension of reality? I'm not aware of any study where that's happened. In fact, large populations and other significant worldviews readily include spiritual beings and forces in their accounts of reality. It turns out that the anti-supernatural view of the world is a minority view around the world.

Please don't misunderstand what I'm saying. I think that when you experience pain, you should go see a medical doctor, not a witch doctor. But that doesn't mean that you can't also pray for relief and healing. Naturalism presents the situation as an either-or when it's really a both-and.

To dismiss the claim that spiritual forces or beings exist by saying that we know better than that now is to fall victim to what theologian Gregory Boyd calls, "chronocentrism," the assumption that our present worldview is the only valid one. Boyd suggests, "If we modern Westerners cannot 'see' what nearly everyone else outside the little oasis of Western rationalism the last several centuries has seen, then perhaps there is something amiss with our way of seeing."[78]

This barrier doesn't seem very strong because it's based on an assumption that can't support its own weight. Someone should require a better reason for disbelieving in God than merely, "We've moved passed that sort of thing."

## Barrier #2: People needed a God, so they invented one, didn't they?

The premise of this barrier goes back to Ludwig Feuerbach, Sigmund Freud, and Karl Marx. In their own ways, each of these men saw belief in God as a fantasy of our own making. In this fantasy, human beings project their experiences and desires onto a cosmic stage and call it God.

---

[77] Walter Wink, *Naming the Powers: The Language of Power in the New Testament* (Minneapolis: Fortress Press, 1984), 4.
[78] Gregory A. Boyd, *God at War: The Bible and Spiritual Conflict* (Downers Grove: InterVarsity Press, 1997), 18.

Religion, then, isn't related to reality at all. Like a child's imaginary friend, God isn't really there; we only wish he was. Accordingly, religion can be said to function as an "opium of the people" (Marx's famous phrase), offering support to weak people who need to believe in such things to get through the day. But if you're strong, so the thinking goes, then you don't need to believe in those kinds of religious fantasies.

Alister McGrath points out a significant hole in this idea, saying, "it is certainly true that things do not exist because we desire them. But it does not follow from this that, because we desire something, it does not exist."[79] In other words, we can't conclude that God isn't real simply because some people would like for God to be real.

To see how inadequate the line of thinking in this barrier really is, consider what happens when the same logic is used in the other direction. Let's say that there are many people who don't wish for God to be real. For them, the idea of God might carry unpleasant overtones of ethics, accountability, and judgment. Should we conclude, then, that God must be real because some people don't want him to be real? Of course not. Yet, that's the same logic behind what's being proposed in this barrier to belief.

So, it turns out that saying people invented a God-figure because they wanted one cuts the other way too. It could be said, on the same basis, that people who don't believe in God are projecting their own needs, experiences, and desires onto a cosmic stage and saying that there's nothing and no one there.

Czeslaw Milosz is a Polish poet who endured the hostilities of Nazism and Stalinism before winning the Nobel Prize in Literature in 1980. He believed that Marx was wrong when he claimed that religion is the opium of the people. According to Milosz, "A true opium of the people is a belief in nothingness after death, the huge solace of thinking that for our betrayals, greed, cowardice, and murders we are not going to be judged."[80] Could it be that the real opium of the people today is

---

[79] Alister McGrath, *Intellectuals Don't Need God and Other Modern Myths* (Grand Rapids: Zondervan, 1993), 96.
[80] Czeslaw Milosz, "The Discreet Charm of Nihilism," *The New York Review of Books* (November 19, 1998), https://www.nybooks.com/articles/1998/11/19/discreet-charm-of-nihilism/.

disbelieving in God? Perhaps people don't want there to be a God, so they imagine he's not there.

Who's making things up? Who's projecting their beliefs onto the cosmic stage? Is it those who believe in God or those who don't? The answer isn't as obvious as Feuerbach, Freud, and Marx made it seem. For that reason, this barrier doesn't seem very strong.

## Barrier #3: If God existed, then suffering wouldn't exist, would it?

This barrier is known as the problem of evil. Stated in its simplest form, the problem of evil asks, "If God is all-powerful and all-good, then why does evil exist?" The question is set up to yield the conclusion that God doesn't, in fact, exist.

For Bart Ehrman, a formidable New Testament scholar and professor at the University of North Carolina at Chapel Hill, it wasn't necessarily evil that led him to abandon his faith, but suffering. He remembers, "I could no longer explain how there can be a good and all-powerful God actively involved with this world, given the state of things. For many people who inhabit this planet, life is a cesspool of misery and suffering."[81]

David Hume, the famous 18th-century philosopher and religious skeptic, framed the problem this way: "Is [God] willing to prevent evil, but not able? Then he is impotent. Is he able, but not willing? Then he is malevolent. Is he both able and willing? Whence then is evil?"[82]

C. S. Lewis also recognized the problem, calling it the problem of pain. He states the problem succinctly, saying, "If God were good, He would wish to make His creatures perfectly happy, and if God were almighty He would be able to do what He wished. But the creatures are not happy. Therefore God lacks either goodness, or power, or both."[83]

---

81 Bart D. Ehrman, *God's Problem: How the Bible Fails to Answer Our Most Important Question – Why We Suffer* (New York: HarperOne, 2008), 3.
82 David Hume, *Dialogues Concerning Natural Religion,* ed. Martin Bell (London: Penguin, 1991), 108-109.
83 C. S. Lewis, *The Problem of Pain* (New York: HarperOne, 1996), 16.

In its variety of forms, this barrier poses a formidable obstacle for many people. So, what can we say? The broad category for explanations about how both God and evil can exist is called theodicy, and the history of theodicy has given us several possible lines of response.

One response is that pain and suffering can help us grow and mature in ways that would be impossible without them. This is a tact taken by theologian Douglas John Hall. Going back to the biblical portrayal of the Garden of Eden, Hall counters the view that everything was pristine, perfect, and painless there. He identifies four conditions in the Garden that suggest at least the possibility of pain even before the entrance of sin in the world.

The first condition is loneliness. In Genesis 2:18, before the woman is created, it's clear that it isn't good for the man to be by himself. Second, there are limitations in the Garden. There are things that humans can do but shouldn't. There are also things they can't do but try anyway. Both situations present occasions for suffering. The third condition that lends itself to pain in the Garden is temptation. The couple can be seduced to act in ways that don't help them. The fourth condition is anxiety. The couple's ignorance and dependence can make them apprehensive and susceptible to the possibility of pain.[84]

So, Hall concludes, "A degree of pain, it would seem, is necessary to evoke the human potential for nobility, for love, for wisdom, and for depth and authenticity of being. A pain-free life would be a life-less life."[85] To be sure, Hall goes on to distinguish between suffering that enhances life and suffering that eliminates life, but it's sufficient here to note his point that all pain and suffering are not inherently bad.

Another line of reasoning about suffering is proposed by Timothy Keller. Going back to the problem of evil, Keller hypothesizes that God might have good reasons for allowing evil, reasons that we can't understand or even know about from our limited frame of reference. Perhaps God allows evil, despite his disdain for it, because it's producing an otherwise desirable outcome. If that's the case, then the problem of evil

---

[84] Douglas John Hall, *God and Human Suffering: An Exercise in the Theology of the Cross* (Minneapolis: Augsburg Press, 1986), 54-62.
[85] Ibid., 63.

isn't a problem at all. Keller summarizes, "If God has good reasons for allowing suffering and evil, then there is no contradiction between his existence and that of evil."[86]

Keller's approach here has affinities with Hall's reasoning above. Keller cites examples of doctors who might prescribe painful procedures for patients in order to help them, and parents who inflict suffering on their children (in the form of time out or loss of privileges) in the short-term so they can learn a lesson for the long-term. If we stop and think about it, there are many instances where we "allow suffering in someone's life in order to bring about some greater good."[87]

A person might retort that he doesn't see how any good could come from a particular evil event that brought suffering on a specific individual or group. But to claim that there's no possible greater good to come in the future, the person making that claim must assume that he's omniscient and omnipresent, standing outside of time and space, able to see all contingent possibilities from the present moment. But that's not the case. No one has that vantage point. So, Keller rounds off his argument, saying, "To insist that we know as much about life and history as all-powerful God is a logical fallacy."[88]

A third line of reasoning invokes the freewill defense. Why is there evil and suffering in the world? The freewill defense supplies the answer, predictably, that human creatures have the freedom to act, and they do so frequently in ways that are evil (contrary to God's desires or intentions) and so cause suffering. Philip Yancey, a Christian author and journalist, leans in this direction when he says, "Many things happen in this world that are clearly against God's will."[89]

But, notice what this explanation must entail. If you, as a human being, are free to do things that are contrary to what God desires (God's will), then in what sense can it be said that God is all-powerful (or omnipotent)? To ask the question a different way, if you can

---
[86] Timothy Keller, *Walking with God through Pain and Suffering,* reprint edition (New York: Riverhead Books, 2015), 97.
[87] Ibid.
[88] Ibid., 98.
[89] Philip Yancey, *Reaching for the Invisible God: What Can We Expect to Find?* (Grand Rapids: Zondervan, 2000), 66.

thwart God's will with your own God-given freewill, then is God really omnipotent? That question begs the question of what's meant by omnipotence. It also begs the question of whether or not human beings have genuine moral agency.

It's here, on these questions, that philosopher Alvin Plantinga is helpful. Plantinga is deliberate about defining what's meant by the claim of God's omnipotence. He writes, "What the theist typically means when he says that God is omnipotent is not that there are *no* limits to God's power, but at most that there are no nonlogical limits."[90] In other words, God's power is limited in some sense, but illogical questions of whether God could make a square circle or rock so big he couldn't lift it are nonsensical and have never been in the purview of what thoughtful people mean when they talk about omnipotence.

The biblical storyline tells how God freely (sovereignly) created free creatures and gave them important responsibilities within creation. No one forced God's hand or made him do it this way. This was the setup and partnership that he wanted. In this situation, genuine relationships between the Creator and creation were made possible.

Old Testament scholar Terence Fretheim makes clear what this situation means. He says, "God so enters into relationships that God is not the only one who has something important to do and the power with which to do it. Within the very creative process itself, God chooses to share power with the creatures."[91] That act of creation, then, logically places a limit on God's power and forces us to nuance what we mean when we say that God is omnipotent.

Are creatures truly free, then? Do we have genuine moral agency in the world? If God created human beings who are only capable of choosing to do good, it would have eliminated senseless suffering, but it also would have eliminated our freedom. The "choice" to do good under those terms wouldn't be a choice at all. It would be a farce. Freedom would be an illusion, a logical contradiction in which creatures think they're free to choose, but they really aren't. So, Plantinga reasons,

---

90 Alvin Plantinga, *God, Freedom, and Evil* (New York: Harper & Row, 1974), 18.
91 Terence E. Fretheim, *God and World in the Old Testament: A Relational Theology of Creation* (Nashville: Abingdon Press, 2005), 21.

"God can create free creatures, but He can't *cause* or *determine* them to do only what is right. For if He does so, then they aren't significantly free after all. . . . As it turned out, sadly enough, some of the free creatures God created went wrong in the exercise of their freedom; this is the source of moral evil."[92]

It's reasonable to ask why God would create a world where evil was even allowed as a possibility. To that question, the best response seems to be love. Theologian John Sanders explains, "God has entered into an enterprise whereby he seeks the highest good of his creatures and desires to solicit the love of his creatures in freedom."[93]

C. S. Lewis asks and answers the question in a similar way: "Why, then, did God give [humans] free will? Because free will, though it makes evil possible, is also the only thing that makes possible any love or goodness or joy worth having."[94] The freedom we have to love God also includes the freedom to turn away from God. The choice and its consequences are ours to live with.

The key to this final line of reasoning is a reinterpretation of God's omnipotence based on freewill. Because God has chosen to involve free creatures in his creation, he has limited his options, so to speak. God must now act and work within the logical boundaries of the world he chose to make. And God is willing to do so for the sake of love. Portrayed this way, evil and suffering are unwelcome trespassers in God's otherwise and originally good world. As such, a future day of redemption is promised to those who don't give up faith and hope in the present. On that day, there will be no more death, sorrow, crying, or pain (Revelation 21:4).

The problem of evil and suffering is a legitimate problem, a significant barrier to faith for many people. That's why I spent so much time here tracing out some possible responses to it. In the end, though it *is* a barrier, it's not an impenetrable one. Many capable thinkers have

---

92 Plantinga, *God, Freedom, and Evil*, 30.
93 John Sanders, *The God Who Risks: A Theology of Divine Providence*, 2nd edition (Downers Grove: InterVarsity Press, 2007), 45.
94 Lewis, *Mere Christianity*, 53.

shown that it's possible to maintain faith in God despite the presence of evil and suffering in the world.

## Barrier #4: Religion poisons everything, doesn't it?

The phrasing of this barrier comes from the late Christopher Hitchens' book, *God Is Not Great: How Religion Poisons Everything*. The book came out in 2007 and made its way to the New York Times Bestseller list in only three weeks. In the book, Hitchens, an atheist, claims the moral and intellectual high ground over religious believers. He cites instances of religious violence that have occurred around the world.[95] He associates organized religion with violence, intolerance, ignorance, and coercion.[96] He suggests that it might be a form of child abuse for parents to provide their children with religious instruction.[97] Ultimately, according to Hitchens, "*Religion poisons everything*. As well as a menace to civilization, it has become a threat to human survival."[98]

Nothing that Hitchens said is particularly new or novel. He only modernized the sentiments originally put forward at the beginning of the Enlightenment. For example, in 1807, political philosopher Thomas Paine wrote, "The most detestable wickedness, the most horrid cruelties, and the greatest miseries that have afflicted the human race, have had their origin in this thing called revelation, or revealed religion."[99] The idea that religion poisons everything has been around for a while. So, what can be said about it?

One response is that religion is not the only ideology capable of producing violence and fanaticism. Politics, for one, is completely capable of producing those outcomes. Many people associate suicide bombings with religious fanaticism, but a comprehensive study conducted by Robert Pape, a professor of political science at the

---

95 Christopher Hitchens, *God Is Not Great: How Religion Poisons Everything* (New York: Twelve Books, 2007), 18-28.
96 Ibid., 56.
97 Ibid., 217-228.
98 Ibid., 25.
99 Thomas Paine, *The Age of Reason* (1807), 147. Online: http://klymkowskylab.colorado.edu/Readings/Thomas%20Paine%20-%20The%20Age%20of%20Reason.pdf

University of Chicago, found that most suicide bombers are acting more politically than religiously. After compiling a database of every suicide attack in the world from 1980 through 2003, Pape concluded, "The data show that there is little connection between suicide terrorism and Islamic fundamentalism, or any one of the world's religions."[100] This flatly contradicts their portrayal by Hitchens and others as acts of religious violence. Furthermore, nearly 25% of the 315 total attacks were perpetrated by a group that is totally opposed to religion. Nearly 96% of the attacks, Pape says, "could have their roots traced to large, coherent political or military campaigns."[101]

Political fanaticism certainly has the power to turn violent, as much, if not more so, than religious fanaticism. Dinesh D'Souza, former president of The King's College in New York City, comments, "Religion-inspired killings simply cannot compete with the murders perpetrated by atheist regimes."[102] How so? He explains, "Taken together, the Crusades, the Inquisition, and the witch burnings killed approximately 200,000 people. . . . Even so, these deaths caused by Christian rulers over a 500-year period amount to only 1 percent of the deaths caused by Stalin, Hitler, and Mao in the space of a few decades."[103] This means that there's no reason to concede the moral high ground to Christopher Hitchens when he attacks religion on the grounds of violence and commends atheism as the path to peace. Specific forms of religious belief *can* lead to violence, but other ideologies are not innocent of that same charge.

The second way to respond to the line that religion poisons everything is to admit that bad things have been done in the name of religion, but also to insist that a religion shouldn't be evaluated by the actions of those who have most maligned it.

In his book, *Speaking of Jesus*, Carl Medearis recounts numerous conversations he's had with people around the world about Jesus. He

---

[100] Robert Pape, *Dying to Win: The Strategic Logic of Suicide Terrorism* (New York: Random House, 2005), 4.
[101] Ibid.
[102] Dinesh D'Souza, *What's So Great About Christianity* (Carol Stream: Tyndale House, 2007), 219.
[103] Ibid.

often found that talking about Christianity brought up all sorts of baggage for a lot of people. So, rather than trying to wade through and explain away all the faults and failures in Christianity's past, Medearis decided to focus his message on Jesus. He says, "I believe that the gospel [about Jesus] and the religion of Christianity can be two different messages. Even opposed on some points. When we preach Christianity, we have to own it. When we preach Jesus, we don't have to own anything."[104]

With Jesus, there's no secret scandal to cover up, no abuse to ignore, and no fraud to deny. Jesus called on people to turn from sin and invited them into the love of God. Filled with grace and speaking truth, Jesus offered renewed hope and abundant life to those who had little of either. It's no wonder why people who were nothing like him liked him. That's what Medearis means when he says we don't have to own anything when it comes to Jesus.

It must be acknowledged that people have done things in Jesus' name that Jesus wouldn't want to be associated with. However, the truthfulness of Jesus' message shouldn't be evaluated by the actions of those who acted contrary to it, even if they thought they were somehow acting in concert with it. About this point, Alister McGrath adds that "historical and personal associations do not have any necessary or direct bearing on whether a position is true or not."[105] People and institutions may let us down, but that doesn't mean that Jesus isn't who he said he was.

The barrier that religion poisons everything, then, shouldn't be something that keeps a person from believing. It claims more than it can support, and it can't stand up to rational scrutiny.

## Barrier #5: I need to be absolutely certain, don't I?

This barrier usually emerges for people after the other barriers have been overcome. Belief is becoming a reasonable option, but something – a thought – shows up and slows down the process. The thought is

---
104 Carl Medearis, *Speaking of Jesus: The Art of Not-Evangelism* (Colorado Springs: David C. Cook, 2011), 47.
105 McGrath, *Intellectuals Don't Need God*, 69.

often a question, something like, "But how can I be *sure* about this?" And by "sure," the person usually means "certain."

Is certainty possible? Sometimes it is, but most of the time it isn't. For example, "Do you feel pain in your arm right now?" is a question that you can answer with certainty. You either feel pain right now, or you don't. But, what about a different kind of question, like, "Will the airplane make it to its destination?" Or, what about, "Is the food safe to eat?" You can feel confident about your answers to those questions, but you can't be certain. You can't be certain because the answers to those questions involve other people and situations that aren't under your control.

The same thing is true for another kind of question: "Do your friends really like you?" Again, you can be confident but not certain about your answer. And yet, in all of these scenarios, we don't let a lack of certainty stop us, do we? We still travel; we still eat; we still have friends. But we don't have certainty, and that's okay.

It's not that we have blind faith, which is "a condition in which critical reason has been abandoned and any contradictory evidence reflexively dismissed."[106] We aren't just going to believe anything we're told. Instead, we proportion our faith based on each issue's importance and the quality of our reasons. For important issues about which we have good reasons for believing as we do, we have higher degrees of confidence. For other issues about which have lower quality reasons for believing as we do, we have lower degrees of confidence. That's what rational people do. John Stackhouse explains how this works. He says, "We believe something (to use one sense of the word 'believe') and we believe *in* something or someone (to use the other sense) because we possess what we have judged to be good (enough) grounds to do so."[107]

Basically, all we can do is find and claim what we believe to be the best explanation for what we see and experience happening in us and around us. We're unlikely ever to be able to prove our conclusion, or experience absolute certainty about it, but it works and makes sense to us as an inference to the best possible explanation based on the

---
106 Stackhouse, *Need to Know,* 210.
107 Ibid., 208.

preponderance of evidence available to us. Most of the time, that's the best anyone can do. And most of the time, that's enough.

Gregory Boyd acknowledges this situation and recognizes that we live in a world that is "filled with complexity, ambiguity, and unanswerable questions." Instead of pushing people to produce feelings of certainty, he invites them to embrace a "kind of faith that accepts . . . that there is no need for [absolute certainty], so long as we have *reason enough* to place all our trust in Christ."[108] He helpfully shifts the target from certainty to a confidence that's based on probability.

Blaise Pascal, a French mathematician and philosopher in the 17th century, understood all of this. He knew that cold logic could only take a person so far when answering the question of God's existence, so he insisted, "The heart has its reasons, which reason does not know." To that end, he framed the decision about faith in terms of making a wager on a game, not doing a science experiment. Here are the terms of the wager, according to Pascal: There either is a God or there isn't; reason alone will not solve the matter for you. A game is being played where heads or tails will turn up. You must wager. Consider what happens if you wager that God exists: If you win, you win everything. If you lose, you lose nothing. Which way would *you* wager?

Of course, Pascal knew that we can't believe that which we don't find believable. But his wager applies to those on the fence of faith, held back by their desire for an absolute certainty that isn't possible. Our lives always demand some level of risk. So, according to John Stackhouse, "the wise person is the one who does not seek certainty but seeks instead *adequate* reason to believe the best [option] available."[109]

## What We Covered in This Chapter

In this chapter, I acknowledged and addressed five of the most prevalent barriers that keep people from believing in God. Keep in mind that we have not yet made our way to Jesus or Christianity yet.

---

108 Gregory A. Boyd, *Benefit of the Doubt: Breaking the Idol of Certainty* (Grand Rapids: Baker Books, 2013), 32.
109 John G. Stackhouse, Jr., *Humble Apologetics: Defending the Faith Today* (New York: Oxford University Press, 2002), 107.

We have only been talking about the existence of God in general up to this point. It turns out that thinking we've outgrown our need for God is akin to chronological and cultural elitism. The claim that people invented God is inconclusive because it could just as easily be stated in the other direction. Also, the existence of suffering doesn't eliminate the possibility of the existence of God. There are several ways to make sense of that problem. Religion doesn't, in fact, poison everything, and religions shouldn't be evaluated by the actions of their worst participants. And, finally, confidence rather than certainty is the goal because that matches how we actually live our lives.

With these barriers addressed, it's time to move forward in our conversation. Up to this point, we've looked at why we believe what we do. We've talked about why religion won't go away. And we've identified and responded to persistent barriers to belief. In the next chapter, we'll look at the only options we have when it comes to answering the question of whether or not God exists.

# CHAPTER 5
## What Are the Options?

MANY PEOPLE TODAY suffer from option overload, or what author Alvin Toffler has called "overchoice." The modern world has opened up more access to opportunities, information, and options than ever before. For some people, that's a good thing. They now have choices to make that weren't available to them only a few centuries ago. For other people, the number of choices they have to make is overwhelming and sometimes paralyzing.

The menu at McDonald's illustrates the situation. When the McDonald brothers opened the first McDonald's restaurant in 1940, they had only nine items on the menu. In 2013, McDonald's had 145 items on the menu. If you've ever been to a McDonald's and had to wait in line behind someone who couldn't decide what to order, the person in front of you was likely experiencing a moment of option overload.

Sheena Iyengar, a business professor at Columbia University, has researched this phenomenon. In one study, she set up samples of different jams in a store. Sometimes she would have 24 jams available to sample; other times, there would only be six jams available to sample. She wondered which scenario would lead to more jam sales. The results showed that while the larger group of jams drew more people to her table, the smaller group of jams drove more people to make a purchase. According to Iyengar, "30 percent of the people who had seen that small assortment decided to buy jam, but only 3 percent bought a jar after seeing the large assortment."[110] Her study perfectly demonstrates the problem of overchoice.

To many people, approaching the topic of religion might feel like they're looking at a menu with too many options. It can seem confusing and overwhelming. But it doesn't have to be that way. When it comes to the question of whether God exists, there aren't an endless number of answers; there are only three: yes, no, and I don't know. Granted, things can get more complicated as we consider what each of those answers might entail, but it's still a good place to start.

## Option #1: No, God doesn't exist.

Atheism is the belief that God doesn't exist. The root word of atheism is "theism," which derives from the Greek word *theos,* meaning God. Theism means belief in the existence of God. But when the "a" is used as a prefix, it means "not" or "without." So, atheism literally means to not believe in the existence of God.

The earliest civilizations and societies mostly took the existence of God (or the gods) for granted. Jan Bremmer, a professor of Religious Studies in the Netherlands, points out in his article for *The Cambridge Companion to Atheism* that "atheism never developed into a popular ideology with a recognizable following" among ancient Greeks and Romans.[111] Atheism started as a movement with the rise of modernity.

Gavin Hyman, a professor at the University of Lancaster in the UK, clarifies the link between atheism and modernity, saying that "atheism developed as an intellectual phenomenon, increasing in respectability and wider [adoption] as modernity itself developed."[112] This isn't surprising from our current vantage point because, as Hyman notes, "modernity itself is, at its heart, an atheistic edifice."[113] In other words, many of the conclusions arrived at in the modern period were built on

---

110 Sheena Iyengar, *The Art of Choosing* (New York: Twelve, 2010), 187.
111 Jan N. Bremmer, "Atheism in Antiquity," in *The Cambridge Companion to Atheism,* ed. Michael Martin (New York: Cambridge University Press, 2007), 11.
112 Gavin Hyman, *A Short History of Atheism* (New York: I.B. Tauris, 2010), 18.
113 Ibid.

atheistic assumptions. The two movements mutually reinforced each other.

As modernity spread, atheism started capturing the imaginations of intellectual leaders and cultural elites in Western Europe. Interestingly, atheism has remained a popular option for people with similar standing in Western culture today. According to the Pew Research Center, the number of people who identify themselves as atheists is slowly increasing in the United States. Between 2007 and 2014, the number of self-identified atheists in the United States rose from 1.6 percent to 3.1 percent of the population. The research also found that the people who identify themselves as atheists are more likely to be white males who are highly educated.[114]

## *Reasons for Atheism*

There are many different reasons why someone might not believe in God (we covered a few of them in the last chapter). The person may be reacting against the presence of suffering. For example, in his book, *Why I am Not a Christian,* atheist historian Richard Carrier cites suffering as a conclusive reason for believing that God doesn't exist. He says, "if *I* had the means and the power, and could not be harmed for my efforts, I would immediately alleviate all needless suffering in the universe."[115] So, he concludes that God doesn't exist because God doesn't eliminate suffering.

Another reason why someone might be an atheist is to distance himself from people he thinks are unintelligent or hypocritical. For example, in his book, *The End of Christianity,* pastor-turned-atheist John Loftus says, "In my world, miracles do not happen. What world are *you* living in? The odds of a resurrection, from my experience, are 0

---

[114] Michael Lipka, "10 Facts About Atheists," June 1, 2016. Online: https://www.pewresearch.org/fact-tank/2016/06/01/10-facts-about-atheists/. However, further research conducted by the Pew Research Center in 2017 found that 10% of Americans do not believe in any higher power or spiritual force. Online: https://www.pewresearch.org/fact-tank/2018/04/25/key-findings-about-americans-belief-in-god/
[115] Richard Carrier, *Why I Am Not a Christian: Four Conclusive Reasons to Reject Faith* (Richmond: Philosophy Press, 2011), 18.

percent."[116] The obvious implication of his statement is that he's living in the real world while others, who believe in things like miracles, are living in a fantasy world.

The person might also be an atheist because he's convinced that there isn't enough evidence to believe that God exists, or that the evidence can be explained without reference to God. Bill Nye articulates this position when he says, "Every . . . aspect of life that was once attributed to divine intent is now elegantly and completely explained in the content of evolutionary science."[117] While he overstates his case about how completely evolutionary science has explained our world, Nye doesn't believe that a divine being or supernatural occurrence is necessary to explain anything about the world in which we live.

There are, of course, other reasons why someone might disbelieve in God, but what's interesting is when atheists talk about their own journeys toward atheism. They usually tell their stories in terms of courage, maturity, and freedom. They were the ones who were courageous enough to ask the hard questions, stare the truth in the face, and see that God isn't really there after all. And now, with God out of the picture, they're liberated from religious rules and regulations, free to grow up and make something of themselves without reference to anything or anyone else.

But Charles Taylor calls their bluff when they tell that story. He notes that atheism isn't just about science. For many atheists, it's also about a feeling of accomplishment and superiority. Taylor insists that many people who leave belief in God for unbelief have bought into (or believed) the idea that unbelief is "the stance of maturity, of courage, of manliness, over against childish fears and sentimentality."[118] In other words, the atheist sees himself as an adult in his thinking while believers in God are stuck in their childish ways. That's part of atheism's appeal in our secular age.

---

116 John W. Loftus, *The End of Christianity* (Amherst: Prometheus Books, 2011), 79.
117 Bill Nye, *Undeniable: Evolution and the Science of Creation* (New York: St. Martin's Press, 2015), 282.
118 Taylor, *A Secular Age*, 365.

## Reasons Against Atheism

Atheism also has several shortcomings that must be addressed. The first is the issue of meaning. Simply put, if there is no God, then life is rendered meaningless. Some atheist thinkers will disagree with this statement and insist that life without God still has meaning. Jerry Coyne, a biologist and professor at the University of Chicago, is a good example. According to Coyne, "although the universe is purposeless, our lives aren't. . . . We make our own purposes, and they're real."[119]

I take his point. So, it's not that life has no meaning without God. It's that life has no *inherent* meaning without God. And that fact is acknowledged by every atheist thinker I can find. When Stephen Jay Gould, an evolutionary biologist, was asked about the meaning of life, he answered, "We cannot read the meaning of life passively in the facts of nature. We must construct these answers for ourselves."[120] In other words, meaning in life isn't essentially built into life itself. The only meaning in life is the meaning that we assign to it. Not surprisingly, Gould goes on to insist that the project of constructing meaning is liberating for people.

William Provine, another evolutionary biologist, summarized his views in a debate at Stanford University. He confidently stated, "There are no gods, no purposes, and no goal-directed forces of any kind. There is no life after death. . . . There is no ultimate foundation for ethics, no ultimate meaning in life, and no free will for humans, either."[121]

David Barash taught psychology at the University of Washington and put the matter starkly, saying that we should stop deluding ourselves with the "infantile illusion" that a personal God exists. Instead, we

---

119 Jerry A. Coyne, "Ross Douthat is On Another Erroneous Rampage Against Secularism," *The New Republic,* December 26, 2013. Online: https://newrepublic.com/article/116047/ross-douthat-wrong-about-secularism-and-ethics

120 Stephen Jay Gould, "The Meaning of Life: The Big Picture," Life Magazine, December 1988. Online: https://www.maryellenmark.com/text/magazines/life/905W-000-037.html

121 Darwinism: Science or Naturalistic Philosophy? A Debate Between William B. Provine and Phillip E. Johnson at Stanford University, April 30, 1994. Online: http://www.arn.org/docs/orpages/or161/161main.htm

should face "the reality that life in general and our individual life in particular is inherently meaningless."[122]

These people can say that facing a meaningless life is the mark of courage, maturity, and freedom, but the failure to acknowledge that life has inherent meaning is a problem for atheism. Out of all living creatures, human beings are the ones who seek meaning, value, and purpose for their lives. But when God is removed from the picture, inherent meaning is lost. That's why atheism often leads directly to nihilism, the "skeptical and pessimistic ideology that sees all existence as meaningless."[123] When people are repeatedly taught and told that they came from nothing and end up nowhere, we shouldn't be surprised when people don't see any meaning, value, or purpose for their lives (or the lives of others).

Leo Tolstoy, a Russian writer who died in 1910, called attention to the problem. He lamented that when he pressed science for an answer to the meaning of life, he was told, "You are a little lump of something randomly stuck together. The lump decomposes. The decomposition of this lump is known as your life. The lump falls apart, and thus the decomposition ends, as do all your questions." But, Tolstoy insisted, "to say that [my life] is a particle of infinity not only fails to give it any meaning but destroys all possible meaning."[124]

Another reason to question atheism is that important questions about the origins of our world are left unanswered. Author Brian McLaren offers a few questions to consider: "Where does everything come from? Why does something exist rather than nothing? Why did the Big Bang bang when it did and how it did? Why did conscious, intelligent life develop?"[125]

---

122 David P. Barash, *Through a Glass Brightly: Using Science to See Our Species as We Really Are* (New York: Oxford University Press, 2018), 26.
123 Christopher Muscato, "Existential Nihilism vs. Atheism." Online: https://study.com/academy/lesson/existential-nihilism-vs-atheism.html
124 Leo Tolstoy, *Confession*, Translated by David Patterson (New York: W. W. Norton, 1983), 42.
125 Brian D. McLaren, *Finding Faith: A Self-Discovery Guide for Your Spiritual Quest* (Grand Rapids: Zondervan, 1999), 86.

Stephen Jay Gould, one of the biologists mentioned above, attempts to answer the question about the origin of life by saying, "We are here because one odd group of fishes had a peculiar fin anatomy that could transform into legs for terrestrial creatures." However, he acknowledges that if you "wind back life's tape to the dawn of time and let it play again . . . you will never get humans a second time."[126] In other words, everything that had to happen perfectly for life to be established on earth just happened to happen perfectly. Theists believe this observation points in the direction of Intelligent Design.

Richard Dawkins has a more elaborate theory about our origins. He says, "On one planet, and possibly only one planet in the entire universe, molecules that would normally make nothing more complicated than a chunk of rock, gather themselves together into chunks of rock-sized matter of such staggering complexity that they are capable of running, jumping, swimming, flying, seeing, hearing, capturing and eating other such animated chunks of complexity."[127]

But it still seems obvious to most people that something can't come from nothing. And even if one puts forward the theory that matter originated from energy in the form of photons, that theory still begs the question about the original source of that energy.[128] Perhaps that's why Stephen Hawking, the late professor of mathematics at Cambridge, acknowledged, "It is difficult to discuss the beginning of the universe without mentioning the concept of God."[129]

Basic logic demonstrates that a chain of events in the physical world can't go infinitely backward. There must have been a first cause from outside the chain of events that at least put the chain of events into motion. If a series of dominoes are falling over, there must have been

---
126 Stephen Jay Gould, "The Meaning of Life." Online: https://genius.com/Stephen-jay-gould-the-meaning-of-life-annotated
127 Richard Dawkins, *The God Delusion,* reprint edition (New York: Mariner Books, 2008), 411.
128 Sara Slater, "Where Did the Matter In the Universe Come From?" Online: http://curious.astro.cornell.edu/the-universe/101-the-universe/cosmology-and-the-big-bang/general-questions/570-where-did-the-matter-in-the-universe-come-from-intermediate
129 Stephen Hawking, ABC Television 20/20 Interview, 1989. Online: http://hyperphysics.phy-astr.gsu.edu/Nave-html/Faithpathh/hawking.html

a force from outside the series of dominoes that knocked over the first domino. This has been understood since as far back in time as Aristotle. Theists insist that God is the first cause.

The third reason to question atheism is that it does away with a reliable standard of justice and goodness. Brian McLaren emphasizes this point. He says, "Atheism leaves no standard beyond ourselves or outside ourselves to look up to, to appeal to, to help us discern what is really and ultimately right."[130] But every sane person knows that some things are wrong for people to do, even if some people feel like those things are the right things to do.

For example, in 2019, Tisha Sanchez suffocated her 8-year-old son. Why did she do that? She said that demons told her to sacrifice him.[131] No one came to her defense and said that she was just doing what she felt was right. Instead, people said that what she had done was wrong. Morality wasn't a matter of preference in her case; morality was embedded in reality. And everyone knew that Tisha Sanchez had done the *wrong* thing.

C. S. Lewis equates this universal sense of right and wrong with the Law of Nature. He insists that when we argue for fairness or justice or progress, we're acknowledging that there's a proper standard of behavior which hasn't been met. According to Lewis, "The moment you say that one set of moral ideas can be better than another, you are, in fact, measuring them both by a standard, saying that one of them conforms to that standard more nearly than the other."[132] Where does that standard come from?

It won't do to say that our views of right and wrong are only culturally conditioned impulses. That's the approach some people take. They point out that what counts as acceptable behavior and what doesn't can differ from culture to culture.[133] However, there's a difference between

---

130 McLaren, *Finding Faith*, 95.
131 Sara Coello, "Irving mom said demons told her to sacrifice 8-year-old son, police say," *Dallas News*, June 24, 2019. Online: https://www.dallasnews.com/news/crime/2019/06/24/irving-mother-charged-capital-murder-8-year-old-sons-slaying
132 Lewis, *Mere Christianity*, 25.
133 For example, William Graham Sumner, *Folkways* (Chicago: Ginn and Company, 1906).

particular social conventions and the universal values that undergird those conventions. A social convention might be which side of the road to drive on or what kinds of clothes are acceptable to wear. Those things will undoubtedly differ from one culture to the next, but the values of order and appropriateness are cross-cultural. In other words, we might designate different things as right or wrong, but we don't disagree that there *is* such a thing as right and wrong.

Lewis suggests, "If anyone will take the trouble to compare the moral teaching of, say, the ancient Egyptians, Babylonians, Hindus, Chinese, Greeks, and Romans, what will really strike him will be how very like they are to each other and to our own."[134] The reason for this striking similarity, according to Lewis, is that these moral values, this universal sense of right and wrong, came from God.

Francis Collins agrees with Lewis about how we arrived at our sense of right and wrong, and he offers this illustration: "If I'm walking down the riverbank, and a man is drowning, even if I don't know how to swim very well, I feel this urge that the right thing to do is to try to save that person. Evolution would tell me exactly the opposite: preserve your DNA. Who cares about the guy who's drowning? He's one of the weaker ones, let him go. . . . And yet that's not what's written within me."[135]

Atheism insists that God doesn't exist, and atheists have reasons for believing the way they do. But there are also reasons to question whether such a position is intellectually viable, socially productive, and existentially satisfying.

## Option #2: I don't know if God exists.

Agnosticism is the position of someone who doesn't know (and sometimes doesn't care) if God exists. The root word of agnosticism is *gnosis,* the Greek word for knowledge. As with atheism, the "a" that's included at the beginning of the word means "not" or "without." So, agnosticism literally means to be without knowledge.

---

134 Lewis, *Mere Christianity,* 19.
135 Francis Collins, "The Question of God: Other Voices," PBS.org (undated). Online: https://www.pbs.org/wgbh/questionofgod/voices/collins.html

A person can be agnostic about any subject. If you're asked for your opinion about a book that you haven't read, you could say that you're agnostic about it. That reply would be correct because you've never read that book and you don't have the knowledge needed to give your opinion. But, in religious conversations, agnosticism refers to the question of God's existence.

In the religious sense, an agnostic is someone who either doesn't know if God exists or doesn't believe it's possible to know if God exists. The first person to call himself an agnostic was an English biologist named Thomas Henry Huxley in 1869. Huxley wanted to distinguish his belief from the beliefs of atheism, pantheism, deism, and theism. He explains, "[Those other beliefs] were quite sure they had attained a certain 'gnosis'; had more or less successfully solved the problem of existence; while I was quite sure I had not, and had a pretty strong conviction that the problem was insoluble."[136]

From that first use of the term, however, agnosticism "has become a label signifying anything from a noncommittal open-mindedness about religion or 'spirituality' to a reluctant or skeptical attitude towards any kind of phenomenon where an attitude of belief is possible."[137] For example, Bertrand Russell was willing to call himself an atheist in some situations and an agnostic in others, depending on the audience.[138]

Robin Le Poidevin, a professor of metaphysics in England, suggests that a sliding scale would be useful to understand agnostic attitudes about God's existence. At one end of the scale is absolute confidence that God exists. At the other end is absolute confidence that God doesn't exist. Le Poidevin says that "it seems reasonable to label the area around the middle of this scale 'agnosticism,' allowing it to shade gradually

---

136 Thomas Henry Huxley, "Agnosticism," in *Christianity and Agnosticism: A Controversy* (New York: Humboldt Publishing, 1889), 20-21. [full article: pp. 9-29]. Online: https://archive.org/stream/agnosticism00variuoft/agnosticism00variuoft_djvu.txt
137 Egil Asprem, *The Problem of Disenchantment: Scientific Naturalism and Esoteric Discourse, 1900-1939* (Albany: SUNY Press, 2014), 289.
138 Bertrand Russell, "Am I an Atheist or an Agnostic?," (1947). Online: http://www.personal.kent.edu/~rmuhamma/Philosophy/RBwritings/iAtheistOrAgnostic.htm

(with no determinate cut-off points) into theism in one direction and atheism in the other."[139]

This sort of sliding scale would reinforce the findings of the Pew Research Center, which found that 31 percent of self-identified agnostics said they don't know or aren't certain when it comes to the question of God's existence. Another 20 percent of the group felt fairly certain that some kind of God exists, and another 41 percent didn't believe in God at all.[140] Maybe that's why Brian McLaren suggests that agnosticism is "a popular option for all those who . . . find atheism too great a leap of faith or too extreme a solution to the problems they see in theism."[141]

## *Types of Agnosticism*

Agnosticism is difficult to categorize because agnostics have a variety of views and reasons for holding those views. Nevertheless, an attempt to clarify three different types of agnosticism might prove to be helpful here.

First, there is strong agnosticism, also known as closed agnosticism. This view says that it isn't possible for human beings to know whether or not God exists because we aren't capable of accurately judging the available evidence.

Second, there is weak agnosticism, also known as open agnosticism. This view says that God might exist, and it's probably possible to find out, but the evidence that's currently available hasn't been convincing enough.

Third, there is apathetic agnosticism, also known as ignorant agnosticism. This view says that the whole question of God's existence is trivial, unimportant, inconsequential, and not worth putting forth the energy required to form an opinion.

---

[139] Robin Le Poidevin, *Agnosticism: A Very Short Introduction* (New York: Oxford University Press, 2010), 9.
[140] Pew Research Center, "Agnostics," from The Religious Landscape Study. Online: https://www.pewforum.org/religious-landscape-study/religious-family/agnostic/
[141] McLaren, *Finding Faith*, 101.

These differences make agnostics an eclectic group with a wide range of reasons for settling in their current position.

## *Reasons for Agnosticism*

The reasons for atheism that were listed above might just as easily be used as reasons for agnosticism. As a reminder, those reasons include the problem of evil and suffering, not wanting to be associated with unintelligent people, and being convinced that there isn't enough evidence to believe in God.

In addition to those reasons, a few more reasons can be added here that – in my experience – are more closely aligned with agnosticism than atheism. One reason why someone might identify as an agnostic is that he wants to avoid the sense of guilt that comes from falling short of religious expectations. This makes sense because many agnostic people have a religious background. The idea is straightforward: If I distance myself from certain religious beliefs and values, then I'm free to say and do whatever I want to say and do, without reference to those religious beliefs and values. This idea also connects with the narrative of liberation from external expectations that was mentioned earlier.

Beyond feeling guilty for not living up to specific religious standards, converting to agnosticism would also free a person from feeling like a hypocrite. In this sense, the liberation is not from external expectations but from internal expectations. One agnostic person told me about how she left her faith behind in college. She said that she would party on Friday and Saturday nights, and then show up at church on Sunday mornings. She started feeling like a phony. Her roommates teased her about being a hypocrite. They said she was fake. Finally, she decided to stop going to church on Sundays. The feelings of hypocrisy went away, and she never made her way back to church. Her beliefs adjusted to accommodate her lifestyle choices and free her from feeling like a hypocrite.

Another reason why someone might become an agnostic is that he doesn't want to endorse some of the beliefs or behaviors associated with a particular religion. This is the reason given by one blogger for his deconversion from Christianity. After becoming a Christian in college, he took a job in a new city and met a kind, intelligent, faithful Hindu man. The blogger says he abandoned Christian faith because he "could not swallow the fundamental, core message of the religion." What was the core message of Christianity that he couldn't swallow? In his words, that message was: "Believe in Christ or burn in hell." While that is most certainly not the core message of Christianity, it was enough to move the blogger to his current position of agnosticism.[142]

The blogger's story matches the conclusions reached by John Barbour, a religion professor at St. Olaf College. Barbour examined the process of deconversion and explained, "Often it was perceiving the unacceptable moral consequences of holding certain beliefs that led to a deconversion. Or a church's attempt to stifle intellectual doubts or criticisms was experienced as a threat to both freedom of thought and personal responsibility."[143] Findings from the Pew Research Center support Barbour's conclusions. In their interviews, they found that 71 percent of agnostics question a lot of the religious teachings they hear, and almost half don't like the positions churches have taken on social issues.[144]

## *The Illusion of Neutrality*

Agnosticism is a middle-ground position that's staked out by some people who have thought deeply about the issues and other people who don't want to think about the issues at all. It allows people to remain flexible with their own beliefs and values, not really getting involved in debates about who's right and who's wrong. In that way, agnosticism seems like a religious version of Switzerland, neutral.

---

142 Dave Morse, "Why I'm Not a Christian – A Manifesto on Agnosticism," Medium.com (June 3, 2016). Online: https://medium.com/@davemorse/why-im-not-a-christian-a-manifesto-on-agnosticism-ad1768b8aa8c
143 John D. Barbour, *Versions of Deconversion: Autobiography and the Loss of Faith* (Charlottesville: The University Press of Virginia, 1994), 56.
144 Becka A. Alper, "Why America's 'Nones' Don't Identify with a Religion," *Pew Research Center,* August 8, 2018. Online: https://www.pewresearch.org/fact-tank/2018/08/08/why-americas-nones-dont-identify-with-a-religion/

But it's seeming neutrality can be misleading. Gregory Boyd says that "agnostics fail to see that to choose *not* to commit to any belief about spiritual matters is itself a choice to *commit* to a belief about spiritual matters."[145] In other words, the claim that God is unknowable is, in fact, a claim to know the real truth about God. And, if that's the real truth about God, then the agnostic is saying (without saying it) that everyone who thinks God is knowable is wrong.

Consider the familiar story about blind men touching and describing an elephant, a favorite among agnostics. The story, which has been around for thousands of years and told across many cultures, tells about a group of blind men's first encounter with an elephant. Each man feels a different part of the elephant's body and describes it. The man who grabs the tail compares it to a rope. The man who touches the leg compares it to a tree trunk. The man who feels the tusk compares it to a spear. And so on.

The moral of the story in the Western world is that different religions have each only grasped a small part of the truth about God, and no religion can claim to have grasped the whole truth. This idea is behind the "Coexist" bumper sticker that many agnostics display on their cars. But Timothy Keller points out a flaw in the moral of the story. He explains, "The story is told from the point of view of someone who is not blind. . . . How could you possibly know that no religion can see the whole truth unless you yourself have the superior, comprehensive knowledge of spiritual reality you just claimed that none of the religions have?"[146]

Lesslie Newbigin, a British theologian who spent forty years as a missionary in India, also called out the supposed humility of this story about the blind men and the elephant. He says, "There is an appearance of humility in the protestation that the truth is much greater than any one of us can grasp, but if this is used to invalidate all claims to discern the truth it is in fact an arrogant claim to a kind of knowledge which

---

145 Gregory A. Boyd, *Benefit of the Doubt: Breaking the Idol of Certainty* (Grand Rapids: Baker, 2013), 46-47.
146 Timothy Keller, *The Reason for God: Belief in an Age of Skepticism* (New York: Riverhead, 2008), 9.

is superior to the knowledge which is available to [everyone else]."[147] In other words, intellectual humility is a good thing, but it shouldn't be used to reduce everything to the level of opinion or relativize every claim to truth. When that happens, it's no longer intellectual humility, but intellectual arrogance in disguise.

When Rumi, a 13th-century teacher of Sufism, told a version of this story, he concluded by saying, "If each [man] had a candle and they went in together, the differences would disappear."[148] In his version, the men weren't blind; they couldn't see because the room was dark. It's interesting to consider, then, that the Gospel of John actually presents Jesus as a kind of candle, the light of the world that illuminates the darkness and allows people to truly see.

## Option #3: Yes, God exists.

Theism is the belief that God exists. As I said above, theism comes from the Greek word *theos,* which means "God." When the suffix "ism" is used, it indicates that the word is being used to represent a specific system of behavior, philosophy, or belief. In this case, theism is the belief in God or gods. If we probe a little deeper into theism, we find certain varieties that force us to distinguish things a little more precisely. But I'll get to that in due time.

It should be noted that most people in most civilizations throughout the history of the world have believed that a God or gods existed. Emil Brunner points this out, saying, "Men have always asked . . . 'In what way shall we think of God?' but never before, 'Is there a God?'"[149] Looking at the natural world, with all of its beauty, power, and complexity, naturally led to the conclusion that something or someone bigger than us made us. Even when we encounter chaos, the chaos can still serve as a reminder that we are finite and mortal in contrast to a God who is infinite and immortal. For theists, then, it's implausible

---

147 Lesslie Newbigin, *The Gospel in a Pluralist Society* (Grand Rapids: Wm. B. Eerdmans, 1989), 170.
148 Wikipedia contributors, "Blind men and an elephant," *Wikipedia, The Free Encyclopedia,* https://en.wikipedia.org/w/index.php?title=Blind_men_and_an_elephant&oldid=902836194.
149 Brunner, *Our Faith,* 4.

to think that nothing produced something and that no-life somehow produced life.

## *Reasons for Theism*

It might be implausible to believe that something came from nothing, but is it plausible to believe that there's a God, an intelligent being or spiritual force, behind all that we see? Many philosophers and scientists say there is. A few of the essential reasons for thinking so are helpful to consider here.

First, the world had a beginning. This reason is commonly referred to as the Kalam Cosmological Argument. Expressed in logical terms, the argument proceeds in three steps: 1) Everything that begins to exist has a cause of its existence. 2) The universe began to exist. 3) Therefore the universe has a cause of its existence. According to philosopher William Lane Craig, this argument should "demonstrate the existence of a first cause which transcends and creates the entire realm of finite reality."[150] In simpler terms, nothing cannot produce something. Craig adds, "That the universe began to exist is true enough, but that it should begin to exist utterly uncaused out of nothing is too incredible to be believed."[151]

Another reason for believing that God exists is that the world appears to be designed. When we look through a telescope or a microscope, or even in the mirror or out the window, we see features of the world that are strikingly complex, intricate, and interrelated. Philosopher C. Stephen Evans observes that experiences like these lead many people to believe that God or gods exist because, in his words, "Intricate order that supports some good seems purposive; . . . Apparent design suggests a designer."[152] This line of reasoning is known as the teleological argument, from the Greek word *telos,* which means purpose, end, or goal.

---

150 William Lane Craig, *The Kalam Cosmological Argument* (Eugene: Wipf & Stock, 1979), 64.
151 Ibid., 142.
152 C. Stephen Evans, *Why Christian Faith Still Makes Sense: A Response to Contemporary Challenges* (Grand Rapids: Baker Academic, 2015), 43.

## Chapter 5: What Are the Options?

A famous illustration of the teleological argument was developed by William Paley in 1802. Suppose you found a watch on the ground. No one would assume it has always been there in just that way. Instead, the proper assumption would be that someone, somewhere, at some time had formed the watch for a specific purpose of telling time. Paley concludes, "Every indication, every manifestation of design, which existed in the watch, exists in the works of nature."[153]

Timothy Keller offers another illustration. He asks us to imagine a prisoner who has been sentenced to be executed by a firing squad. Ten of the best sharpshooters are brought in to enact the sentence and execute the prisoner. But something unusual and unexpected happens. Even though the shooters were only ten feet away from the prisoner when they fired at him, every one of their shots missed him. While it's *possible* that they all missed by chance or accident, it's more reasonable to think that they all meant to miss him. That would be the most likely explanation for what happened. In the same way, when Keller thinks about our universe, he says, "It is improbable that all the physical constants just happened to be perfectly tuned for life on their own. It would be more reasonable to conclude it was something intended or designed."[154]

The fine-tuning of our world was recognized by renowned scientist Isaac Newton, who commented that the "beautiful system of the sun, planets, and comets, could only proceed from the counsel and dominion of an intelligent being."[155] Additionally, Alvin Plantinga points out how, in more recent times, "Astrophysicists and others have noted that several of the basic physical constants – the velocity of light, the strength of the gravitational force, and of the strong and weak nuclear forces – must fall within very narrow limits if intelligence is to develop."[156] What does all this mean? It means that our world is set up perfectly to allow for our existence.

---

153 William Paley, *Natural Theology* (Philadelphia: H. Maxwell, 1802).
154 Keller, *Making Sense of God*, 219.
155 Quoted in Alvin Plantinga, *Where the Conflict Really Lies: Science, Religion, and Naturalism.* (New York: Oxford University Press, 2011), 193.
156 Ibid., 194.

Beyond the cosmological argument and the teleological argument, another reasons why theists believe that God exists is the moral argument. The moral argument says there are things that we believe are wrong for people to do, no matter how they feel about them or what they think about them. For example, I don't know anyone who isn't repulsed when they hear the story of Nathaniel Bar-Jonah, a convicted child molester, serial killer, and suspected cannibal. It's thought that he served his victim's remains in burgers, spaghetti, chili, and casseroles at neighborhood cookouts.[157]

If you cringed when you heard that, it's because you have a sense of morality. Most human beings have an innate desire to align ourselves with goodness and truth. This impulse makes sense within the framework of a world that was created by a God to whom we are accountable. It makes no sense, however, in a world that came about by chance, coincidence, or accident.

While no single argument for the existence of God is conclusive by itself, in the end, when all the evidence is weighed and arguments are considered, theists believe that "the total evidence available from every region of human experience" points to the existence of God.[158]

## *Reasons Against Theism*

When atheists try to refute the cosmological argument, they resort to some questionable lines of thought. For example, Lawrence Krauss, a theoretical physicist who taught at Arizona State University and Yale, says that something *can* come from nothing. He writes, "We have discovered that all signs suggest a universe that could and plausibly did arise from a deeper nothing."[159]

Meanwhile, Francis Crick, one of the biologists who discovered the structure of DNA, went far beyond the realm of biology when

---

157 Wikipedia Contributors, "Nathaniel Bar-Jonah," *Wikipedia, The Free Encyclopedia,* https://en.wikipedia.org/w/index.php?title=Nathaniel_Bar-Jonah&oldid=895896621.
158 C. Stephan Evans, *Why Believe? Reason and Mystery as Pointers to God* (Grand Rapids: Wm. B. Eerdmans, 1996), 24.
159 Lawrence M. Krauss, *A Universe from Nothing: Why There Is Something Rather Than Nothing* (New York: Simon and Schuster, 2012), 183.

he seriously suggested that "organisms were deliberately transmitted to the earth by intelligent beings on another planet."[160] For Crick, the idea of God is so far-fetched that he needed to invoke the idea of aliens to explain our existence. That isn't science; it's science fiction.

When it comes to the teleological argument, an atheist has two main rebuttals. One way to respond is to say that what appears to be the fine-tuning of the universe by an intelligent being is, in reality, only the product of a series of random coincidences. So, Steven Weinberg, a Nobel Prize-winning physicist, insists that human life is "a more-or-less farcical outcome of a chain of accidents."[161] In other words, there's no design or purpose to our world or our lives; we're only here by accident.

The other response is to suggest what's known as the "multiverse thesis." This theory suggests that there's an infinite number of parallel universes, all spawning from the initial Big Bang. Given enough time, and considering the sheer number of possible universes, it's not surprising that eventually, one universe (ours) would develop the features necessary to sustain and support life.

But the multiverse theory has a significant problem for scientifically-minded people. The problem is that it isn't based on science. Paul Davies, an English physicist, points this out. He says, "The multiverse theory may be dressed up in scientific language, but in essence it requires the same leap of faith [as believing in God]."[162] Scientists George Ellis and Joe Silk warn that the multiverse has more in common with speculation than real science.[163] Maybe that's why Alan Guth, a

---

160 F.H.C. Crick and L.E. Orgel, "Directed Panspermia," *Icarus*, vol. 19, Issue 3 (July 1973), 341-346. Abstract online: https://www.sciencedirect.com/science/article/abs/pii/0019103573901103. See also, Francis Crick, *Life Itself: Its Origin and Nature* (New York: Simon and Schuster, 1981).
161 Steven Weinberg, *The First Three Minutes: A Modern View of the Origin of the Universe* (New York: BasicBooks, 1977), 154.
162 Paul Davies, "A Brief History of the Multiverse," *The New York Times* (April 12, 2003). Online: https://www.nytimes.com/2003/04/12/opinion/a-brief-history-of-the-multiverse.html
163 Stephanie Margaret Bucklin, "Is the Multiverse Physics, Philosophy, or Something Else Entirely?", *Astronomy* (January 18, 2017). Online: http://astronomy.com/news/2017/01/what-is-the-multiverse

physicist at M.I.T., admits, "I'm a fan of the multiverse, but I wouldn't claim it's true."[164]

These sorts of rebuttals lead Ravi Zacharias to conclude, "Science just does not have knowledge of the beginnings in the genuine sense of the term. It cannot answer the *how*, much less the *why* of there being something rather than nothing."[165]

## Types of Theism

Here's where theism gets a little more technical because we have to get a bit more specific. When it comes to religious systems that endorse the belief that God exists, there are three main versions to consider.

### *Pantheism*

First, there's pantheism. The word comes from combining *pan* (meaning "all") and *theos* (meaning "god"). Strictly speaking, it should be noted that pantheism doesn't fit the technical definition of theism because pantheists don't believe in a God who is distinct from creation. Instead, pantheists believe that the universe created itself and reality consists of an undifferentiated oneness (also known as monism). According to pantheism, everything is God, and God is everything. Paul Harrison, the founder of the World Pantheist Movement, explains, "Pantheism . . . does not believe in a God who even partly transcends time and space. The focus of reverence is the Universe itself, right here, right now in this present time, all around us and in us. We are each part of the awe-inspiring whole and it is part of us."[166]

New Age guru Eckhart Tolle teaches a form of pantheism in his book, *A New Earth*. He writes, "Even a stone, and more easily a flower or a bird, could show you the way back to God, to the Source, to

---

164 Dan Vergano, "Big Bang Discovery Opens Doors to the 'Multiverse,'" *National Geographic* (March 19, 2014). Online: https://news.nationalgeographic.com/news/2014/03/140318-multiverse-inflation-big-bang-science-space/
165 Ravi Zacharias, *The Real Face of Atheism*, revised edition (Grand Rapids: Baker, 2004), 43.
166 Paul Harrison, *Elements of Pantheism: A Spirituality of Nature and the Universe*, 3rd ed. (Shaftesbury: Element Books, 2013), 7.

yourself. . . . Its essence silently communicates itself to you and reflects your own essence back to you."[167]

Typical of most New Age pantheistic teaching is the idea that you can be transformed by discovering your true identity, which is divinity. The highest goal is to lose yourself in the knowledge that you and everyone (and everything) else is part of God.

However, because of this goal, pantheism lacks a category for evil and the capacity to deal with it. If a person embodies part of God, then how can another person justifiably critique anything that person does. One person might not like what another person does, but there are no grounds to say that their actions are wrong. Morality and values are reduced to matters of preference. To put it more bluntly, if God is all and all is God, then it follows that the "rapist and rape victim, murderer and murdered, child molester and molestee . . . are all equally expressions of the One [God]."[168] If that idea doesn't sit well with you, the pantheist will say it's because you haven't discovered your true identity yet. When you do discover your true identity, then you'll accept everyone and everything equally.

So, the inability to identify evil poses a major problem for pantheism. But, as C. S. Lewis remarked, "If you do not take the distinctions between good and bad very seriously, then it is easy to say that anything you find in this world is part of God."[169]

## *Polytheism*

Polytheism is the belief that many gods exist, not just one. The word comes from combining *poly* (meaning "many") and *theos* (meaning "god"). In ancient times, many – if not most – societies were polytheistic. The pantheon of divine beings in those cultures included sky gods, water gods, and fertility gods, among others. In his book, *The Evolution of God,* journalist Robert Wright mentions a Mesopotamian document from 2,000 years before the time of Jesus that lists gods

---

167 Eckhart Tolle, *A New Earth: Awakening to Your Life's Purpose* (New York: Penguin Books, 2005), 26.
168 McLaren, *Finding Faith,* 117.
169 Lewis, *Mere Christianity,* 45.

with various titles, including gardener, valet, bailiff, secretary, and even hairdresser.[170] Sometimes one god out of the many would be considered supreme.

It's thought that polytheistic religions began as a form of nature worship in which the forces of nature were worshiped because of their undeniable power to sustain life or cause death. As time passed, those forces were personified, given names, and worshiped accordingly. In modern times, the most notable polytheistic religion is Hinduism. While Hindu scholars disagree about the total number of gods and goddesses, the number is estimated to be around 330 million.[171]

But polytheism raises plenty of questions, particularly about the hierarchy of the gods in relation to each other. Is one supreme? Is one the original? Are all of the gods equal in status? In Hinduism, Rama and Krishna are both worshiped. But they're identified as avatars (or incarnations) of the higher god Vishnu. Vishnu is part of the Hindu triumvirate, along with the gods Brahma and Shiva. But even among the three, Vishnu is considered by many to be the greatest. All of this begs the question of why worshipers wouldn't simply bypass Rama, Krishna, and all the others, and offer worship only to Vishnu.[172]

Because polytheism isn't clear about its answers to questions like these, it fails to be a viable option for many people in our society.

## *Monotheism*

Monotheism is the belief that there's one God. The word comes from combining *mono* (meaning "one") and *theos* (meaning "God"). Today, the vast majority of religious believers in the world belong to one of the three monotheistic religions: Judaism, Christianity, and Islam.

---

[170] Robert Wright, *The Evolution of God* (New York: Little, Brown and Company, 2009), 86.
[171] L. T. Jeyachandran, "Challenges from Eastern Religions," in *Beyond Opinion: Living the Faith That We Defend*, ed. Ravi Zacharias (Nashville: Thomas Nelson, 2007), 82. Essay on pp. 79-105.
[172] Online: https://www.bbc.co.uk/religion/religions/hinduism/deities/vishnu.shtml

## Chapter 5: What Are the Options?

Many religious scholars point out that monotheism was a doctrine that slowly developed throughout Israel's history, in the pages of the Old Testament. For example, Karen Armstrong says that "the first unequivocal statement of monotheism in the Bible" occurs in the second part of the book of Isaiah (Isaiah 40-55).[173]

However, there's a strand of monotheism that goes all the way back to the act of creation itself, when God is said to have created and populated the heavens and the earth (see Genesis 1:1f). This view is what New Testament scholar N. T. Wright has called "creational monotheism." According to Wright, first-century Jews, in-line with their predecessors, believed that "there was only one god, and this god had made the world. Moreover, he remained active within it."[174] This belief set Jews, and later Christians, apart from pantheism and polytheism (discussed above), as well as deism.

Deism is the idea that God created the world but has been uninvolved with its daily operations since that time. Deism highlights God's transcendence and preserves the distinction between God and creation (which pantheism fails to do). But it neglects God's immanence and involvement in creation (which monotheism seeks to emphasize).

It should be noted that monotheism doesn't necessarily rule out the existence of other spiritual beings in the universe. Monotheism just assigns those other beings to a secondary status. They're not divine; they're created. Gregory Boyd explains this subtle but significant distinction. "[C]reational monotheism," he says, "affirms that there are a multiplicity of other gods [or spiritual beings], but only one is eternal, only one is Creator . . . [A]ll others have their being and power only by virtue of being given it by their Creator."[175]

If there is a God, monotheism seems to make the most sense. Unlike pantheism, it doesn't conflate divinity and humanity. Unlike polytheism, it distinguishes between spiritual forces and the ultimate origin of creation. Monotheism also provides a basis for believing that

---

173 Karen Armstrong, *The Case for God* (New York: Knopf, 2009), 45.
174 N. T. Wright, *The New Testament and the People of God* (Minneapolis: Fortress Press, 1992), 250.
175 Boyd, *God at War*, 121.

life has purpose, distinguishing between good and evil, and believing that help is available to us when we need it.

## Not the Same

After surveying these options, it should be clear why it doesn't make sense to say, as some people do, that all religions are the same, or that all religions are equally true. Anyone who says that obviously doesn't understand either religions or truth. However, there's another idea that different religions are just different paths up the same mountain. At the top, they'll all meet and embrace each other, appreciating the fact that they were all on the same journey all along. But Stephen Prothero, professor of religion at Boston University, reduces this idea to wishful thinking. He writes, "this sentiment, however well-intentioned, is neither accurate nor ethically responsible."[176] It turns out that everyone can't be right.

But we shouldn't be confused about why people disagree when it comes to belief. After all, we're talking about God. And, as Rob Bell poetically says, "when we talk about God, we're talking about our brushes with spirit, our awareness of the reverence humming within us, our sense of the nearness and the farness, that which we know and that which is unknown, that which we can talk about and that which eludes the grasp of our words, that which is crystal-clear and that which is more mysterious than ever."[177]

## What We Covered in This Chapter

In this chapter, I unpacked the only three ways a person can answer the question of whether God exists: yes, no, and I don't know. Atheism says that God doesn't exist. Atheists often portray themselves as holding the intellectual high ground, but things aren't that simple. When atheists talk about how life started, they have to resort to faith to make their claims. Agnosticism claims not to know if God exists,

---

[176] Stephen Prothero, *God Is Not One: The Eight Rival Religions That Run the World* (New York: HarperOne, 2010), 3.
[177] Rob Bell, *What We Talk About When We Talk About God* (New York: HarperOne, 2013), 91.

and sometimes doubts whether it's even possible to know if God exists. It comes across as a neutral position, but that neutrality is an illusion. Believing that you're right about something means you believe that people who don't agree with you are wrong. Theism says that God exists, and they put forward arguments based on the beginning of the world and the appearance of design. But there are different strands of theism. Pantheism says that everything is God and God is everything. Polytheism says that many different gods exist. Monotheism says that only one God exists, and it maintains a distinction between God and creation. When it comes to all of these differences, it doesn't make sense to conclude that everyone is right about what they believe.

For the rest of this book, then, we'll focus our attention on the person who claimed to embody all that we talk about when we talk about God. Not only did he claim to embody it, but he claimed to do so in a unique, unprecedented, and never duplicated way. That person is Jesus, and it's worth listening to what he had to say.

# INTERLUDE
## Why Isn't God More Obvious?

A QUESTIONER ONCE asked Bertrand Russell what he would say if he found himself standing before God on judgment day. What reason would he give when God asked him why he hadn't believed. Russell replied, "Not enough evidence, God! Not enough evidence!"

Many people find themselves in a similar predicament to that of Bertrand Russell. They recognize the scientific shortcomings and they acknowledge the experiences of transcendence, but they don't necessarily believe in God because they feel like God hasn't left enough traces of his existence to be sure about it.

Norwood Russell Hanson, a notable 20th-century philosopher, pointed to the lack of what he called "observable evidence" as a reason for his unbelief. What kind of observable evidence was he looking for? He suggested, "If the heavens cracked open and [a] Zeus-like figure . . . made his presence and nature known to the world," then that would count as evidence.[178] That, he said, would make theism thinkable. But would it really?

Everyone knows that events are open to many different interpretations. When a strange looking object is seen in the sky, some people say it must be aliens while other people say there's no way it could be aliens. The reason for the discrepancy is that an event doesn't usually assign an interpretation to itself. Assigning an interpretation to the event is left up to the people who witness it happening or hear about it later.

---

178 Norwood Russell Hanson, *What I Do Not Believe and Other Essays* (Dordrecht: Reidel, 1971), 322.

Also, our values, vested interests, and vantage points affect our interpretations. If we start from the premise that a particular cause isn't possible, then we'll only consider lines of interpretation that don't include that particular cause. So, it's possible that two different people who witness the scene that Hanson describes above might have two completely different interpretations about what happened. One might say it was a hoax or a strange cloud formation. Another might say it was a demon or perhaps God. Even an incredible, miraculous event wouldn't settle the matter of God's existence beyond dispute.

This point was demonstrated several times during Jesus' life. For example, in Luke's Gospel, Jesus tells a story about two men who had died. One man was taken to Paradise (a place of rest); the other man was taken to Hades (a place of agony). The man in Hades recognized his error and begged to go back somehow to warn his brothers and make sure they didn't end up there with him. But the man was told, "If they won't listen to Moses and the prophets, they won't listen even if someone rises from the dead" (Luke 16:31). The story implies that some people won't believe no matter how overwhelming the evidence is, because there will always be another way to interpret it.

Another example is found in John's Gospel. Jesus had healed many people and performed many miracles. "But," John comments, "despite all the miraculous signs Jesus had done, most of the people still did not believe in him" (John 12:37). Many people saw amazing things happen, but they still didn't believe that Jesus was who he claimed to be. Some people, however, saw those same things and did believe.

A third example is found in Mark's Gospel. As Jesus breathed his last breath and died on the cross, there were at least two different reactions based on different interpretations of that moment. One reaction was that of the political and religious authorities. They believed they had rightfully executed a blasphemer who had caused nothing but trouble for them. The other reaction was that of a Roman officer. He believed they had wrongfully executed the Son of God who had done nothing but good for people. According to Mark's Gospel, "When the Roman officer who stood facing [Jesus] saw how he had died, he exclaimed, 'This man truly was the Son of God!'" (Mark 15:39).

## Interlude: Why Isn't God More Obvious?

Given the flexibility that's built into the process of interpreting events, philosopher Paul Moser suggests, "If you demand a universally convincing undeniable manifestation of God, you should consider whether that is really a viable demand."[179] In other words, what you're asking for might not be possible.

Granted all of that, what if the focus of the question shifted from undeniable evidence to believable evidence? In his book, *Letters from a Skeptic*, Gregory Boyd shared letters that he and his skeptical dad sent back and forth to each other as they discussed the believability of Christian faith. One of the questions that Boyd's dad posed gets to the heart of this topic. He asked, "Why does [God] toy with mankind, teasing us with evidence that's good enough to make us uncomfortable, but never coming directly out and making Himself clear?"[180]

Philosophers and theologians have been wrestling with this question for centuries (it's definitely not a new question), and the responses they've offered can be grouped into four general categories.

### Reason #1: God's Ways

One reason why God might not be as obvious as we'd like him to be is that God is quieter than we think he should be. Philip Yancey says, "it almost seems that God prefers to work through means that to the human observer seem least supernatural."[181] In this view, God is more like an introvert than an extrovert. He is reserved and keeps his distance. He likes to work behind the scenes rather than on the stage. It's like God opens up space for us to live our lives "without constant intrusion, interference, or domination."[182] Perhaps he prefers listening over speaking. Maybe he likes to whisper more than he likes to shout.

This was the prophet Elijah's experience in the Old Testament. A powerful wind came, but God wasn't in it. An earthquake came, but

---

179 Paul K. Moser, *Why Isn't God More Obvious?* (Norcross: RZIM, 2000), 33.
180 Gregory A. Boyd and Edward K. Boyd, *Letters from a Skeptic: A Son Wrestles with His Father's Questions about Christianity* (Colorado Springs: Life Journey, 2003), 119.
181 Philip Yancey, *Rumors of Another World: What on Earth Are We Missing?* (Grand Rapids: Zondervan, 2003), 188.
182 McLaren, *Finding Faith*, 139.

God wasn't in it. A fire came, but God wasn't in it. Then, finally, God spoke to him in a quiet whisper (1 Kings 19:11-13). Because absence makes the heart grow fonder, it's possible that when we sense God's absence, "we can achieve a deeper, more profound appreciation of God's presence."[183]

## Reason #2: God's Goals

Another reason why God isn't more obvious to us might be that God wants us to develop into mature, wise, responsible human beings. As any good parent knows, if God smothered us and overwhelmed us all the time, it would stunt our growth. C. S. Lewis hinted as this idea in *The Screwtape Letters*. In that story, an older demon is coaching a younger demon about how to disrupt the work that God is doing in a man's life. The older demon delights that "the Irresistible and the Indisputable are the two weapons which the very nature of [God's] scheme forbids Him to use. . . . [God] wants them to learn to walk and must therefore take away His hand."[184]

Dallas Willard agrees with Lewis, suggesting, "From the very beginning God intended that we should have fellowship with him, but also that there should be some distance, so that we might be free and capable of choosing and deciding what we would be."[185] Along this line of thinking, God's hiddenness is actually evidence of his love, even if it doesn't always feel that way. The Psalm writer asked, "O Lord, why do you stand so far away?" (Psalm 10:1). Perhaps the answer to his question is that God wants to develop our character more than he wants to remove our challenges.

## Reason #3: Our Focus

A third reason why God isn't more obvious might be because we're distracted. We have our own schedules and priorities to think about. Those things fill our minds and consume us. We're busy thinking about

---

183 Moser, *Why Isn't God More Obvious?*, 5.
184 C. S. Lewis, *The Screwtape Letters*, reprint edition (New York: HarperCollins, 1996), 39-40.
185 Willard, *The Allure of Gentleness*, 65.

the next meal, or the next weekend, or the next vacation. A crowded minded simply doesn't have room to think about or recognize the ways that God might be active in the world and in our lives.

Or, maybe we're suppressing the evidence of God that *is* available to us because we're not open to changing certain lifestyles or habits that have become familiar and comfortable. In that case, Brian McLaren suggests, "God could be putting evidence of his existence all around us, and we would be oblivious."[186] If people want to experience God's presence, they can. But if they don't want to experience God's presence, they don't have to. James, the brother of Jesus, endorsed this idea when he said, "Come close to God, and God will come close to you" (James 4:8).

## Reason #4: Our Sin

The last reason why God might not be as obvious as we would like is because of our sin. We aren't in Eden anymore. There was a time when human beings lived every moment with an acute awareness of God's presence. They knew he was the source and sustainer of life, and apart from him there would be nothing. But that was then, and this is now.

When sin entered the world, it brought distortion, disease, and death with it. It caused our current condition where we're inclined to call evil "good" and good "evil." Even our hearts can deceive us, and our best intentions can lead to disastrous results. Sin has blinded us from seeing the many ways that God is involved in the daily affairs of our lives.

Emil Brunner highlights this reason, saying, "Our madness, haughtiness, irreverence – in short, our sin, is the reason for our failure to see the Creator in His creation."[187] The Psalm writer also channeled this idea when he said, "Only fools say in their hearts, 'There is no God.' They are corrupt, and their actions are evil; not one of them does good!" (Psalm 14:1-2).

---

186 McLaren, *Finding Faith*, 139.
187 Brunner, *Our Faith*, 18.

## A Combination of Reasons

There could be many other reasons why God isn't more obvious, but these four are the most popular responses given by philosophers and theologians through the years. It's unlikely that a single reason is sufficient to answer the question. More likely, the answer is contained in some combination of these four reasons.

When Gregory Boyd answered his dad's question, he appealed to reasons similar to these and concluded, "There's plenty of solid evidence for anyone who wants to believe, but enough faith is required to still render it a moral choice and not a coerced decision."[188] It seems clear that if a person honestly looks for God, that person will find what he's looking for.

---

188 Boyd and Boyd, *Letters from a Skeptic*, 125.

# CHAPTER 6
# Who Was Jesus?

JEFF COOK IS a lecturer in the philosophy department at the University of Northern Colorado. He's also a Christian. But he didn't arrive at Christian faith through a series of mystical experiences; he was attracted to Christian faith through his sincere study of Jesus. He was drawn by Jesus' personality and convinced that Jesus shows us what God is truly like. As he describes his journey of faith, he says, "When I scan the philosophies about God, when I look for a narrative driving history, when I encounter a personality in my prayers, when I simply ask, 'If there was a God what would it look like?' – they move me toward Jesus."[189]

Jesus is one of the most influential yet enigmatic figures in world history. Though some people believe that Jesus never actually existed (a position known as mythicism), they are a small minority and aren't usually taken seriously. The overwhelming majority of historians acknowledge the historical fact that Jesus existed.

However, to think seriously about Jesus, we have to remove the halo from his head. Unfortunately, in a lot of Christian art and iconography, Jesus glows. He isn't human. He isn't one of us. He strides through crowds unfazed, dishing out his healing powers (or withholding them) for no apparent reason. He seems unmoved, above it all, and above *us* all. But that doesn't reflect the reality. So, Dallas Willard advises, "You have to take [Jesus] out of the category of religious artifacts and holy

---

[189] Jeff Cook, *Everything New: One Philosopher's Search for a God Worth Believing In* (Greeley: Subversive Books, 2012), 60.

holograms that dominate presentations of him in the modern world and see him as a man among men, who moved human history as none other."[190]

## What Do We Know About Jesus?

Even though Jesus never wrote a book, there's a lot we can know about him. The primary sources of information about Jesus' life and teachings are the four Gospels that are included in the New Testament. While the Gospels aren't our only sources of information about Jesus, they are our best sources.

I was on vacation in Wyoming when a man struck up a conversation with me. As we talked, the subject turned to religion. He was a mythicist who didn't think Jesus actually existed. He said that the only historical references to Jesus come from the Bible and they can't be trusted. It took only a few seconds to help him see that he was wrong about that. The truth is, there are several places where Jesus is mentioned in antiquity, though most aren't favorable to him or his cause.

A Roman historian named Tacitus mentioned that Jesus had been crucified under Pontius Pilate during the reign of Tiberius. Tiberius was the emperor of the Roman Empire from 14 to 37 AD, and Pontius Pilate was the prefect (or governor) of Judea between 26 and 37 AD. Those details line up with what the Gospels say happened to Jesus, as well as the timeframe they describe.

Another reference to Jesus from outside the Bible comes from a Jewish historian named Josephus. Josephus describes how Jesus' brother, James, was condemned. That detail supports the claim made by the Apostle Paul in Galatians 1:19 that James, the brother of Jesus, was also a leader in the early church in Jerusalem. There are other references too, from a Roman named Pliny the Younger and the Babylonian Talmud, but these are enough to demonstrate the point that the Gospels aren't

---

190 Willard, *Knowing Christ Today*, 67.

## Chapter 6: Who Was Jesus?

our only sources of information about Jesus, but they are our best sources.[191]

So, what do we know about Jesus? Bart Ehrman provides a basic summary that's accepted as historically valid by most scholars: "Jesus was a lower-class Jewish preacher from the backwater of rural Galilee who was condemned for illegal activities and crucified for crimes against the state."[192] With this concise summary of Jesus' life, Ehrman provides the outer edges of a puzzle that needs to be filled in to make sense.

Jesus grew up in a town called Nazareth as the son of a handyman (Matthew 13:54-55). His dad, Joseph, was a *tekton,* a Greek word that could mean builder, stone cutter, or carpenter, among other things. As he grew up, Jesus learned his dad's trade (Mark 6:3). Nazareth was a tiny town in the region of Galilee. The town was seventy miles north of Jerusalem, twenty miles east of the Mediterranean Sea, fifteen miles west of the Sea of Galilee, and four miles south of Sepphoris, the closest major city. Nazareth was in the middle of everywhere and the middle of nowhere.

Religion was at the center of life for Jesus and his family. The Gospels of Matthew and Luke include genealogies that trace the lineage of Jesus' parents back through King David. That connection taps into a deep memory and persistent hope among Jewish people. David had united the nation and established a monarchy a millennium earlier, and God had promised David a dynasty (2 Samuel 7). Solomon, David's son, built the Temple in Jerusalem but then broke covenant with God and wrecked the monarchy by casting himself as a new pharaoh and Jerusalem as a new Egypt. The monarchy split and eventually fell apart. The Temple was torn down, and the young Jewish leaders were taken away to Babylon in exile.

But the prophets didn't let the dream die. They believed that the God who had set them free in the Exodus would set them free again. It

---
191 Robert E. Van Voorst, *Jesus Outside the New Testament: An Introduction to the Ancient Evidence* (Grand Rapids: Wm. B. Eerdmans, 2000).
192 Bart D. Ehrman, *How Jesus Became God: The Exaltation of a Jewish Preacher from Galilee* (New York: HarperOne, 2014), 1.

would be a new Exodus. And they believed that God would enact this new Exodus through a new son of David who would do better than Solomon had done. This new son of David would serve others instead of being served by them (Isaiah 53).

But the deliverance was delayed. Years turned into decades, and decades turned into centuries. The Temple had been rebuilt, but the absence of God's presence and power was palpable. The Jewish people continued celebrating and anticipating the day when their deliverer would be revealed.

The genealogies of Jesus bring that backstory to the foreground, linking Jesus to David. Unfortunately, we don't know much about Jesus' childhood. According to Luke's Gospel, when Jesus was twelve years old, he went with his family to Jerusalem to celebrate the Passover festival. The family was separated from each other and when his parents found him, Jesus was at the Temple debating with older religious teachers. From there, we're only told that Jesus continued to grow in wisdom, stature, and favor (Luke 2:52).

Years passed, and the Gospels pick up Jesus' story again around 28 AD. The Jewish people were being oppressed by Roman authorities and poorly led by their own religious leaders. Jesus' cousin, John the Baptist, was leading a movement of repentance, preparing the way for God to restore the blessing to Israel and bring a fresh start to the people. John was a zealous figure who attracted large crowds by calling out the religious leaders and baptizing people in the Jordan River. Jesus was among the many who went to John to be baptized, a symbolic act of association and purification. As Jesus emerged from the water, he sensed a new empowerment in his life, and he began his public ministry (Matthew 3:16-17).

## Jesus the Prophet

Later, after John the Baptist was arrested for speaking out against Herod Antipas, the ruler of Galilee, Jesus took the mantle of leadership and continued John's work. However, whereas John's was an announcement of preparation for God's Kingdom, Jesus announced the availability of God's Kingdom (Mark 1:14-16). Jesus challenged people to repent of their sins and invited them to enter God's Kingdom by following him.

Repentance is about considering your current direction and being open to a new one. It's about rethinking everything, acknowledging that you might be wrong, and being willing to adopt a new approach. And God's Kingdom is, in the words of Dallas Willard, "the range of [God's] effective will, where what he wants done is done."[193] Jesus' announcement, then, is a summons for people to turn from sin, follow him, and allow God's purposes and power to rule in their lives.

Jesus attracted large crowds of people as he traveled around the region of Galilee. He went from town to town and village to village but appears to have avoided the bigger cities. Most of the people in the crowds were from the lower class, but there were also wealthy people who joined his group. Those wealthy people provided most of the funding for his ministry (Luke 8:3), but he didn't appear to give them any special treatment.

As he traveled around, Jesus seemed to fit the description of a prophet. N. T. Wright suggests that Jesus' ministry had certain similarities to Israel's earlier prophets. Jesus, he says, was "like the prophets of old, coming to Israel with a word from her covenant god, warning her of the imminent and fearful consequences of the direction she was traveling, urging and summoning her to a new and different way."[194] Also, Jesus identified himself as a prophet on at least one occasion (Mark 6:4). As a prophet, Jesus taught his message through what he said and embodied it through what he did.

### *What Jesus Did*

Let's look first at what Jesus did. For one thing, he healed people of sickness, disease, and demonic possession. He healed people with his words (Mark 3:5). He healed people with his touch (Mark 1:40-42). He

---

[193] Dallas Willard, *The Divine Conspiracy: Rediscovering Our Hidden Life in God* (New York: HarperSanFrancisco, 1997), 25.
[194] N. T. Wright, *Jesus and the Victory of God* (Minneapolis: Fortress Press, 1996), 163.

healed people using physical elements (John 9:6). There are too many examples included in the Gospels to pass this part of Jesus' ministry off as a fluke. When Jesus gives a report of his ministry to his cousin John, he says, "The blind see, the lame walk, the lepers are cured, the deaf hear, the dead are raised to life, and the Good News is being preached to the poor" (Luke 7:22). These actions echo the ones mentioned in Isaiah 35:6 as pertaining to the coming of God's Kingdom. For Jesus, healing people functioned as a foretaste of life under God's rule.

God's power clearly flowed through Jesus in a remarkable, unprecedented way. And, as a result of their encounters with Jesus, broken people were made whole again, and excluded people were included again. Biblical scholar Walter Brueggemann comments that when people were around Jesus, "What they noticed is that life had been strangely and inexplicably changed."[195] That's why the crowds gathered around him. Even people who were nothing like Jesus liked Jesus.

Jesus also broke all sorts of boundaries that had been established within his culture. He regularly ate with people who lived questionable lives. This is significant because sharing a meal signified inclusion and acceptance. Refusing to share a meal with someone meant that they were outside the circle of acceptability. In Jesus' culture, "Meals reflected the social boundaries of a group."[196] So, Jesus was often criticized by religious leaders for hanging out with and eating with irreligious people.

He didn't just go against cultural norms when it came to meals. He also went against tradition when he healed people on the Sabbath day. The Sabbath day was the seventh day of the week (observed on Friday at sundown through Saturday at sundown). The day was to be set apart to God as a holy day of rest. Going all the way back to Moses, breaking Sabbath would result in exclusion from the community of faith (Exodus 31:14). However, in the century before Jesus, well-intentioned religious leader sought to put a boundary line around breaking

---

195 Walter Brueggemann, *The Prophetic Imagination,* 2nd ed. (Minneapolis: Fortress Press, 2001), 105.
196 Marcus Borg, *Jesus: Uncovering the Life, Teachings, and Relevance of a Religious Revolutionary* (New York: HarperOne, 2006, 159.

the Sabbath by defining what types of tasks were considered work. The list was long.

Jesus apparently thought the long list of Sabbath offenses got in the way of God's intention for establishing the Sabbath day in the first place, so he disregarded them. He regularly healed on the Sabbath day, an act which his accusers said was a form of work that violated the command to rest. Jesus' reply went straight to the point: "The Sabbath was made to meet the needs of people, and not people to meet the requirements of the Sabbath" (Mark 2:27). Time and again, Jesus shifted the boundary lines, and operated with greater openness and flexibility than others thought was acceptable. For those who opposed Jesus, it was enough to begin a conversation about how to do away with him (Mark 3:6).

## *What Jesus Said*

Jesus wasn't just a traveling healer and cultural disrupter; he was also an itinerant teacher. James Dunn, a New Testament scholar, points out, "The title accorded to [Jesus] most frequently, if we follow the Gospels themselves, is *teacher*."[197] Sometimes, Jesus chose to teach in a direct way. That's what he did in the Sermon on the Mount (Matthew 5-7). In that "sermon," Jesus taught his listeners how to become what God had always intended Israel to become: a faithful community of generosity, service, and love that leads the world toward God. To that end, Jesus told his followers to work for peace, be the light, help the poor, forgive their enemies, keep their promises, and seek God's Kingdom. According to Jesus, these things would demonstrate a person's true allegiance to God.

There were also other religious teachers at that time; Jesus wasn't the only person with a vision and a message. But Jesus' vision of God's Kingdom clashed with the visions of others. That clash contributed to the heated exchanges he had with the Pharisees and other groups. Their different visions produced different agendas, and the others decided that Jesus was too reckless to be allowed to continue.

---

197 James D. G. Dunn, *New Testament Theology: An Introduction* (Nashville: Abingdon Press, 2009), 54.

But Jesus' teaching had a different ring to it. At the end of the Sermon on the Mount, Matthew's Gospel reports, "When Jesus had finished saying these things, the crowds were amazed at his teaching, for he taught with real authority – quite unlike their teachers of religious law" (Matthew 7:28-29). That should be expected. After all, he wasn't just saying words to generate applause; he was starting a movement to inaugurate God's Kingdom.

Other times, Jesus was more indirect when he taught. One of his favorite ways to teach people was by telling them stories. These stories, also called parables, allowed him to "Tell all the Truth but tell it slant," borrowing a phrase from Emily Dickinson.[198] Parables are fictional stories that evoke a response from listeners because "they challenge us to look into the hidden aspects of our own values [and] our own lives."[199] They bring questions to the surface that we would rather not ask, and they suggest answers that we would rather not hear. That's why Jesus used parables: Sometimes when you tell the truth, you have to tell it slant.

So, Jesus told stories about a farmer scattering seed, a woman searching for a lost coin, a pearl that was extremely valuable, a widow asking a judge for justice, a person helping someone that everyone else ignored, and a son who left home but made his way back. The topics of Jesus' parables aren't threatening; they're ordinary. And that's why their message was able to sneak up on those who heard them.

Most of Jesus' parables started with the phrase, "The Kingdom of God is like...," and ended with a twist from how the situation would've normally been resolved. His trademarked ending was a short phrase: "Whoever has ears let them hear." He was inviting people to think about the story, to ask questions, to dig deeper, to consider the implications of what he'd said. Some people scratched their heads and walked away. But other people couldn't let it (or him) go. That's the power of a parable. It invites you in but leaves the choice up to you.

---

198 Emily Dickinson, *The Complete Poems,* ed. Thomas H. Johnson (Boston: Little, Brown and Company, 1955), 506.
199 Amy-Jill Levine, *Short Stories by Jesus: The Enigmatic Parables of a Controversial Rabbi* (New York: HarperOne, 2014), 3.

So, Jesus was a healer and a teacher. Those were key aspects of his ministry that both attracted and confounded the crowds who came to him. A brief summary of the early days of Jesus' ministry is found in Matthew's Gospel: "Jesus traveled throughout the region of Galilee, teaching in the synagogues and announcing the Good News about the Kingdom. And he healed every kind of disease and illness" (Matthew 4:23).

Here's where many portrayals of Jesus go wrong. They stop here and leave intact the idea that Jesus was a spiritual guru who was ahead of his time. Or maybe he was a harmless guy who was misunderstood by the people in power. But wandering gurus don't typically cause much of a stir, and harmless people aren't usually executed by the state. So, those portrayals of Jesus must be missing something.

## Jesus the Messiah

What's missing in those portrayals are Jesus' claims of uniqueness and exclusivity. John Stott is a pastor who points this out. He says, "The most striking feature of the teaching of Jesus is that he was constantly talking about himself."[200] Jesus said that he was the bread of life, the light of the world, the way, the truth, and the life. He claimed to represent God in a special way.

When considering Jesus, it's hard to miss the fact that "he believed that the fortunes of the people were drawn together on to himself and his own work. He believed . . . that he was the Messiah."[201] The word "messiah," means *anointed one,* and it was the term used by many Jewish people before and after the time of Jesus to refer to the figure who would come and deliver them from their bondage.

The Messiah was the person who would restore the nation to prominence by winning the victory over the current oppressive regime (in this case, that meant the Romans) and establishing a government marked by peace, prosperity, and justice (Isaiah 9:6). Jesus sensed that was his calling, but he also redefined the job description along the way.

---

200 John R. W. Stott, *Basic Christianity,* 2nd ed. (Grand Rapids: Wm. B. Eerdmans, 1971), 23.
201 Wright, *Jesus and the Victory of God,* 481.

Jesus didn't see Rome as the ultimate problem. He saw through Rome to a deeper problem that plagued the people: sin. It was sin, not Rome, that was the real problem. And this didn't mean sin in the sense that they had broken a few arbitrary rules. Sin, in the deep sense that Jesus saw it and talked about it, was the failure to live out the human vocation that was assigned by God in the beginning.

In Genesis 1, human beings were given a role to play in creation. They were made in God's image, which means they were to work within creation on God's behalf, as God's representatives, doing what he would do. In the immediate context of that calling, God had been bringing order out of chaos, creating life with his words, and blessing what was made. The human beings were designed to receive God's life, love, and wisdom and to reflect that life, love, and wisdom into creation. That was the human role, and humans were at peace with God, themselves, each other, and creation as a whole. Everything was very good, which meant that things were as they should be, set up to accomplish the purpose for which they were made.

But the story doesn't stop there. In Genesis 3, the human beings open themselves up to a different way. They listen to another voice. The voice slithers in and promises them life and wisdom beyond their current limitations and wildest dreams. And they bite. At that moment, sin is introduced into the world. Sin means to "miss the mark," and in their case, they missed the mark of living a genuinely human life that was faithful to their original calling.[202] As a result, the life they had turns to death. The innocence they had turns to guilt. The trust they had turns to suspicion. And the vulnerability they had turns to shame.

Sin, in this deeper sense, is the root of our problem because it alienates us from God, ourselves, each other, and creation. Moral failures are only symptoms of our deeper problem. Our deeper problem is that we have cut ourselves off from God's life, love, and wisdom. We have chosen to pursue our own objectives in our own ways. We have exploited creation (including people) rather than cultivating it and helping it flourish.

---

202 Mark E. Biddle, *Missing the Mark: Sin and Its Consequences in Biblical Theology* (Nashville: Abingdon Press, 2005), xiii.

As the Messiah, Jesus came to make things right, to restore what was broken, to point the way to God's Kingdom, and to offer abundant, everlasting life to all who would trust in him and follow him. That's the upside. The downside is that those who reject him and refuse to follow him because they want to continue going their own way will be left to live in a condition of sin and death. That's not because God is mean; it's because God gives people the freedom to make their own choices. As C. S. Lewis said, "There are only two kinds of people in the end: those who say to God, 'Thy will be done,' and those to whom God says, in the end, 'Thy will be done.'"[203]

That message of uniqueness and exclusivity was highly controversial in Jesus' day, as it still is today. There were other groups that had their own visions of what the Kingdom of God should (or would) look like. They opposed Jesus. There were also groups that wanted to maintain their power and authority. They also opposed Jesus. There were groups that wanted to uphold their reputation. They opposed Jesus too. All of those visions, interests, and activities converged during the final week of Jesus' life.

### Jesus' Passion

The final week of Jesus' life is remembered by Christians as Holy Week or Passion Week. Passion, in this sense, comes from the Latin word *passio*, which means "suffering." Jesus' final week – beginning with Palm Sunday and ending with his crucifixion on Friday – was filled with subversive actions and confrontations. Interestingly, the Gospels spend more time on this week of Jesus' life than anything else that happened during the rest of his life.

On that Sunday, spirits were high. Jewish people from all over were gathered in Jerusalem for the start of Passover. It was one of the most important festivals on their calendar because it commemorated the original Exodus from slavery in Egypt and anticipated the time when God would act to deliver them again. Because of that context, it seems

---

[203] C. S. Lewis, *The Great Divorce,* revised edition (New York: HarperOne, 2015), 75.

likely that Jesus deliberately chose Passover as the time when he would finally confront the corrupt powers (religious, political, and personal) head-on.[204]

He rode a donkey into the city while crowds shouted praises and spread palm branches out on the road ahead of him (Mark 11:1-11). The donkey seems like an odd choice of transportation until we understand its significance. Nearly five hundred years earlier, a Jewish prophet named Zechariah had told of a day when Israel's true king would come to Jerusalem riding a donkey. When he arrived, he would bring freedom, peace, and justice to all nations (Zechariah 9:9-12). Jesus rode in on a donkey to link himself with that ancient prophecy. It was a demonstration of who he thought he was. But the good times and high hopes didn't last long.

On Monday, Jesus showed up at the Temple. The Temple functioned as the central symbol of Jewish religious and political life. However, not everyone had a favorable view of what was happening there. The Essene community had withdrawn their support from the Temple because they considered the priests who were charge of it to be illegitimate and corrupt. The Pharisees had started to formulate an alternative theology in which everything the Temple stood for – God's presence, God's promises, God's forgiveness, etc. – could be obtained through other channels without going to the Temple. Other groups saw the Temple as a mechanism for the rich to get richer at the expense of the poor.[205]

With all of that in the background, Jesus showed up at the Temple and shut down the whole operation. He knocked over tables and chased people out. He shouted at them that they had turned the house of prayer into a den of thieves. After that, the Gospels call attention to a renewed and ramped up effort by the priests and religious power brokers to end Jesus' life. They got their wish when Judas, one of Jesus' followers, approached them with an offer. He would lead them to Jesus, and they would pay him money. A deal was struck.

---

204 N. T. Wright, *The Day the Revolution Began: Reconsidering the Meaning of Jesus's Crucifixion* (New York: HarperOne, 2016), 178-179.
205 Wright, *Jesus and the Victory of God*, 412.

## Chapter 6: Who Was Jesus?

On Thursday night, Jesus knew his time was short. He shared a meal (The Last Supper) with his closest followers. After the meal, he took the group out to a garden. The followers fell asleep while Jesus prayed and agonized about the events that would transpire over the next few hours. Judas showed up with a crew of armed guards. They had come to arrest Jesus.

The guards immediately took Jesus to appear before the priests. The priests questioned him and arranged for false witnesses to testify against him. Jesus didn't even try to defend himself. The whole process was rushed, and the verdict was clear long before the group of priests shouted, "Guilty!" (Mark 14:53-64). Jesus was mocked, spit on, and punched repeatedly by the guards as they took him away. Like he taught others to do, Jesus turned the other cheek.

Early Friday morning, Jesus was taken to Pontius Pilate, the Roman governor in the region. He was the one who had the power to declare the death penalty. Pilate listened to the case and concluded that Jesus hadn't done anything wrong. But the priests had stirred up the crowd into a frenzy by that point. The crowds that shouted praises to him on Sunday – only a few days earlier – now shouted for him to be killed. Crowds can be fickle like that.

Pilate granted their wish and issued the order for execution by crucifixion. Again, Jesus was mocked, spit on, and beaten. A crown of thorns was shoved into his scalp. Finally, a tired and bloody Jesus carried his own cross to the site of his execution. Like he taught others to do, Jesus went the second mile.

At 9:00 on Friday morning, Jesus hung on the cross with a sign posted above his head. The sign said, "The King of the Jews." That was his crime. And, like he taught others to do, Jesus spoke words of forgiveness over those who harmed him. The powers of evil won an apparent victory that day. Jesus died around 3:00 in the afternoon. He was buried in a tomb, and the story seemed to end. After all of that, Jesus had been just another failed Messiah. He had made promises to the people and gave them false hope. He and his movement were finished. Jesus clearly wasn't the Messiah because the Messiah wasn't supposed to die at the hands of his enemies.

## The One Thing That Changed Everything

But then something happened that changed the course of history. Christianity wouldn't exist today if what happened hadn't happened. In fact, what happened next is one of the only ways to explain the rise of Christianity at all.

On Sunday morning, the stone that covered Jesus' tomb was rolled away and his body was missing. Only his burial clothes remained. Amidst the speculation about what had happened to his body, the unlikeliest explanation turned out to be the one that made the most sense: Jesus was resurrected from the dead.

It was a surprising, unexpected turn of events. No one, not even Jesus' closest followers, saw it coming. According to N. T. Wright, "Nobody in Judaism had expected the Messiah to die, and therefore naturally nobody had imagined the Messiah rising from the dead."[206] On that Sunday morning, nobody expected there to be no body in the tomb. Dead people stay dead; that's what they do, and that's what they've always done. And yet, as if without missing a beat, Jesus' followers immediately resumed their faith in him as the Messiah. That shift is inconceivable apart from his resurrection.

So, why did people reach the conclusion that Jesus wasn't dead anymore? After all, an empty tomb doesn't really prove anything. Maybe his body was stolen by grave robbers. Maybe it was eaten by wild animals.[207] The empty tomb only means something when it's coupled with Jesus' appearances after his death. Jesus appeared to groups and to his closest followers. He talked with them and ate with them. He wasn't a ghost. He was human but more than human. He still had the marks from his crucifixion, but he could walk through doors. His body had been transformed in a way that later biblical writers struggled to describe.

Without the empty tomb, the appearances could be dismissed as hallucinations. The conclusion that Jesus' followers reached, that Jesus

---

206 N. T. Wright, *Surprised by Hope: Rethinking Heaven, the Resurrection, and the Mission of the Church* (New York: HarperOne, 2008), 47.
207 John Dominic Crossan, *Jesus: A Revolutionary Biography* (New York: HarperOne, 1994), 174.

had been resurrected from the dead, was based on those two things: the empty tomb *and* the appearances. On their own, neither is sufficient to account for what the first Christians believed about Jesus. Together, however, they provide a complete and coherent explanation for what happened.[208]

On that Sunday morning, Jesus and his message were vindicated by God. It's not an overstatement to say that "the event most central to the Christian tradition after the existence of God is the resurrection of Jesus."[209] The judgment against him was wrong. Because of the resurrection, the cross was transformed from a symbol of defeat and death into a symbol of victory and life. Jesus had let sin do its worst to him, and he emerged victorious over it. He had gone through death and come out the other side. Later, the Apostle Paul would say, "[Jesus] disarmed the spiritual rulers and authorities. He shamed them publicly by his victory over them on the cross" (Colossians 2:15).

After forty days of appearances, Jesus commissioned his followers to spread the message that God's Kingdom was available to all people through him and his work. He ascended into the heavenly realm to sit in the seat of authority at God's right hand, promising to appear again in the future to deliver us from death and restore all things to the way they're supposed to be (1 Corinthians 15:23-26). On that day, all who belong to him will be raised to experience and enjoy life with him in a renewed and renovated creation where pain, suffering, and death are fully and finally banished from our experience forever (Revelation 21:1-7).

## The Full Portrait

The portrait of Jesus that has been drawn for us in the Gospels is both comprehensive and compelling. Jesus made bold claims about himself and his mission, but he consistently lived by the same ideals that he taught to others. He doesn't appear to have been a hypocrite or a conman. Indeed, those who knew him best described him as being

---

208 Wright, *Surprised by Hope*, 59.
209 Willard, *Knowing Christ Today*, 132.

without any sin at all (1 Peter 2:22). They said he was full of grace and truth (John 1:14).

Jesus doesn't appear to have been mentally unstable either. He slept when he was tired and wept when he was sad. He attended parties and adjusted his plans. He laughed at jokes and loved his friends. He challenged people with power and comforted those without it. By all appearances, Jesus was firmly in touch with reality.

What's truly inspiring about Jesus is that even though he claimed to be the Lord of all, he made himself the servant of all. He endured death so others could enter life. John Stott says, "The essence of love is self-sacrifice."[210] If that's true (and I think it is), then Jesus fully embodied the essence of love. Who *wouldn't* want to put their trust in someone like that?

## What We Covered in This Chapter

In this chapter, I gave you an overview of Jesus' life. He was from a small town and grew up working for a living and worshiping with his family. He initially followed in John the Baptist's footsteps, but saw his own ministry as going a step further. Jesus announced through his words and actions that God's Kingdom had become available in a new way. He called on people to repent of their sin and follow him. He modeled what he taught others to do. He was a prophet, a healer, and a teacher. But more than that, he claimed to be the Messiah. He broke boundaries, comforted the broken, and challenged the powerful. After he was crucified, his movement was stopped dead in its tracks. But then his tomb was found empty and he appeared to individuals and groups of people over the next forty days. He was vindicated by God and exalted to sit in the seat of authority at God's right hand. If it's true that God is love (1 John 4:16), then it's fair to say that in Jesus we see the embodiment of God.

---

210 Stott, *Basic Christianity*, 44.

# CHAPTER 7
# Are the Sources Reliable?

WHILE MANY PEOPLE are inspired by the Gospels' portrayal of Jesus, they hit a roadblock on the way to believing in him and trusting him with their lives. That roadblock comes from the doubts they feel about the integrity and accuracy of the Gospels' accounts. Before a person can trust Jesus, a different question must usually be explored: "Can the Gospels be trusted?"

Perhaps the stories about Jesus are only legends, tall tales made up and passed down to give hope to hopeless people. Or, maybe the stories about Jesus are only lies, intentional fabrications that were made up by people who wanted to gain or keep power. Those are two of the many proposals that have been put forward in an effort to dismiss what the Gospels say about Jesus. But do those proposals make sense historically? Can the Gospels be trusted, really?

It might help to go back to where we left off at the end of the last chapter. Jesus commissioned his followers (now called apostles, meaning "sent ones") to go out and share the message of Good News with the world. The Good News (or "gospel") is that Jesus is now enthroned and in charge as the true Lord of the world. His life, death, and resurrection has broken the grip of sin and death on humanity, and opened God's Kingdom to all who trust in him. This announcement carried with it the need to teach people about Jesus' life and encourage them to model their lives after his.

As the apostles announced the Good News about Jesus, they saw that "it brought into being a new situation, new possibilities, and a new life-changing power."[211] As the Apostle Paul would later write, the Good News about Jesus unleashed the power of God in people's lives (Romans 1:16). They were filled with boldness and proclaimed the message about Jesus in synagogues and households throughout the region.

## Understanding an Oral Culture

Creating written documents was expensive and, for the most part, unnecessary at that time. It was unnecessary because the message hadn't crossed into new cultures yet. The apostles mostly remained around Jerusalem to provide leadership during those early years of the movement. Plus, most people were illiterate and didn't rely on books; it was an oral culture. Stories and news traveled by word-of-mouth. That's how the message about Jesus spread in the first decades after his resurrection.

As the Good News about Jesus spread, it led to the formation of churches. Most of those churches met in people's homes. Unfortunately, we don't have any documents from churches at that time; there wasn't a New Testament to speak of yet. When people gathered, they spent time in worship, prayer, and study. They learned about and rehearsed the significant details of Jesus' life, primarily through stories and songs.[212]

Because of the oral nature of the stories about Jesus, some scholars have suggested that the information in the stories was changed and embellished as the stories spread. The comparison is often made to the game of telephone in which a person whispers a story into the ear of the person next to him. The story is passed around the group in the same manner until it has made its way around the whole group. Then, the final version of the story is compared with the first version. The two versions are usually very different, and everyone has a good laugh.[213]

---

[211] N. T. Wright, *Scripture and the Authority of God: How to Read the Bible Today* (New York: HarperOne, 2011), 49.
[212] Jonathan Morrow, *Questioning the Bible: 11 Major Challenges to the Bible's Authority* (Chicago: Moody Publishers, 2014), 51-52.
[213] Bart Ehrman, *The New Testament: A Historical Introduction to the Early Christian Writings*, 5th ed. (New York: Oxford University Press, 2012), 72-74.

Chapter 7: Are the Sources Reliable?

But that comparison fails to account for how oral cultures actually worked. Oral cultures placed great value on memorization. It was common for Jewish children, for example, to commit entire books of the Old Testament to memory. That's hard for us to believe today when many of us have a hard time remembering a few phone numbers and birthdays. But that's how it was. Besides that, members of the community would intervene during stories when key details were miscommunicated.

Kenneth Bailey was a research professor in Beirut when he did an extensive study of oral cultures and their process of storytelling. He found that in those cultures if someone was telling a story and they told it wrong – they messed up details, mixed up characters, or misunderstood the point – that person was corrected immediately. Some stories allowed for both continuity and flexibility, but in those cases, Bailey says, "The main lines of the story cannot be changed at all. . . . Within the structure, the story-teller has flexibility within limits to 'tell it his own way.' But the basic story-line remains the same."[214] The telephone game might create laughter at a child's birthday party, but there's no way that people of faith within an oral culture would tolerate the stories about Jesus being changed. That wouldn't have been acceptable to them.

## From Stories to Scripture

As more time passed and persecution of the church increased and the Good News about Jesus crossed cultural lines, it became prudent for the stories to be recorded in written form. So, the four Gospels included in the New Testament – Matthew, Mark, Luke, and John – were written to preserve the stories about Jesus for future generations. However, questions about when the Gospels were written and who wrote them are highly contested.

---

214 Kenneth E. Bailey, "Informed Controlled Oral Tradition and the Synoptic Gospels," in *Themelios* 20.2 (January 1995), 8.

## *Who Wrote the Gospels?*

First, let's look at who wrote the Gospels. Bart Ehrman has a theory about this. He says, "[The Gospels] were not written by Jesus' companions or by companions of his companions. They were written decades later by people who didn't know Jesus, who lived in a different country or different countries from Jesus, and who spoke a different language from Jesus."[215] He also says that the Gospels originally circulated as anonymous documents without titles but were attributed to Matthew, Mark, Luke, and John in the late second century to bolster their authority.[216]

Brant Pitre, a New Testament scholar, says that Ehrman is wrong on both counts. He points out that the biggest problem with Ehrman's theory about the circulation of anonymous Gospels is that *"no anonymous copies of Matthew, Mark, Luke, or John have ever been found. They do not exist. . . .* [T]he ancient manuscripts are unanimous in attributing these books to the apostles and their companions."[217] If the Gospels had circulated for almost one hundred years without a title or author, then we would expect to find some of the anonymous manuscripts or some documents somewhere with contradictory, forged titles. Neither has ever been found to corroborate Ehrman's claim. Instead, the names of Matthew, Mark, Luke, or John are connected to every Gospel that has ever been found as far back as we can go.

Another problem with Ehrman's theory is that the names supposedly chosen for authors wouldn't have bolstered the authority of the Gospels because two of the four Gospels are attributed to people who weren't eyewitnesses of Jesus' ministry. Pitre asks, "If authority is what you were after, why not attribute your anonymous Gospel directly to Peter, the chief of the apostles? Or to Andrew, his brother?"[218] After all, both Peter and Andrew traveled with Jesus and were eyewitnesses to his life

---

215 Bart D. Ehrman, *Jesus, Interrupted: Revealing the Hidden Contradictions in the Bible (and Why We Don't Know About Them)* (New York: HarperOne, 2009), 112.
216 Ibid., 111.
217 Brant Pitre, *The Case for Jesus: The Biblical and Historical Evidence for Christ* (New York: Image, 2016), 15.
218 Ibid., 23.

## Chapter 7: Are the Sources Reliable?

and ministry. If you were picking names that might give a Gospel more credibility or authority, they would be likely choices.

It turns out that half of the Gospels that are included in the New Testament are attributed to people who would most certainly not add an aura of authority to them. Meanwhile, the apocryphal gospels that were left out of the New Testament all took the opposite approach. Those gospels were written much later, and they were attributed to people like Peter, Thomas, Mary Magdalene, and even Judas. That's what it actually looks like when someone is clamoring to boost authority.

Ehrman's other claim is that the Gospels were written by people who didn't know Jesus. He said they weren't Jesus' companions, nor were they companions of his companions. But why does he make that claim? He says that most of Jesus' followers were "simple peasants from Galilee – uneducated fishermen, for example."[219] Because of that, he insists, "they would not have been able to write a Gospel."[220]

This is an overstatement on Ehrman's part. Even though Peter and John are explicitly said to be illiterate in Acts 4:13, not all of Jesus' followers fit that description. Matthew wasn't a fisherman; he was a tax collector, which means it's likely that he would have been able to read and write. R. T. France, an expert on Matthew's Gospel, concluded that "Matthew was better equipped than most by his previous profession for the role of gospel-writer."[221] As one of the few literate followers of Jesus, there doesn't seem to be any reason to deny that Matthew was surely *capable* of writing a Gospel. There also doesn't seem to be any reason to deny the unanimous evidence which claims that he did.

Mark wasn't an eyewitness of Jesus' ministry. He became a Christian in the early stages of the movement after Jesus' resurrection. He initially traveled with his cousin Barnabas and the Apostle Paul as they went around sharing the message about Jesus (Acts 13:4-5). Later,

---

219 Bart D. Ehrman, *Misquoting Jesus: The Story Behind Who Changed the Bible and Why* (New York: HarperOne, 2005), 39.
220 Ehrman, *How Jesus Became God*, 244.
221 R. T. France, *Matthew: Evangelist and Teacher,* reprint (Eugene: Wipf & Stock, 2004), 68.

he separated from Paul and worked alongside Peter. On one occasion, Peter even refers to Mark as a son (1 Peter 5:13), indicating not a biological relationship but a spiritual one.

Mark's connection with Peter is important for validating the trustworthiness of what Mark's Gospel says about Jesus. Mark didn't travel with Jesus, but Peter did. And, remember that Peter was described as illiterate. When Peter wanted to write a letter, he employed a scribe to help (1 Peter 5:12). Peter never wrote a Gospel, but it's thought that he told Mark everything he knew about Jesus. Mark, then, wrote his Gospel based on what he learned from Peter. In that case, "Mark acted as a kind of secretary or scribe who wrote on Peter's behalf and made it his goal to faithfully record what Peter said Jesus did and taught."[222] This description of the origins of Mark's Gospel is what we find in the earliest sources, including a document from a church leader named Papias in 125 AD.

Like Mark, Luke also wasn't an eyewitness of Jesus' life and ministry. He acknowledges that fact at the very beginning of his Gospel (Luke 1:3). Some scholars suggest that Luke's given name was Lucius, and he knew the Apostle Paul and Barnabas from their time in Antioch (Acts 13:1). Others suggest that Luke first met Paul in the city of Troas and went with him from there (Acts 16:6-12). Whatever the case may be, Luke was a physician who traveled and worked alongside Paul (Colossians 4:14).

It's noteworthy that Luke's Gospel seems to be aimed at telling Gentiles (people who aren't Jewish) about Jesus. This was also what Paul felt called to do (Acts 9:15). Perhaps that's why Origen of Alexandria, a leader in the early church, said that Paul praised Luke's Gospel. Luke's Gospel shows that Luke had a strong grasp of the Greek language and was careful to fully investigate the matters he wrote about. Clearly, he was not an illiterate fisherman, and his authorship is universally acknowledged by our earliest sources, including Irenaeus in 180 AD.

John's Gospel claims to be written by an eyewitness of Jesus' life. The writer calls himself "the disciple whom Jesus loved" (John 20:20-24).

---

222 Pitre, *The Case for Jesus*, 45.

That seems like a strange way of speaking about oneself today but using third-person language was customary in ancient writing. The "disciple whom Jesus loved" was closely connected to Jesus and was even said to be seated directly next to him at the Last Supper (John 13:23). Who could that have been? One of Jesus' twelve closest followers was John, the son of Zebedee. It's possible that John was the youngest member of the group, maybe still been a teenager at the time (Mark 3:17). He was also included in Jesus' inner circle, along with Peter and James. Given that John's Gospel is credibly dated to the late first century (more on that below), and John the son of Zebedee was the last of the living apostles at that time, it's leaves him as the most likely candidate to have written it.

But remember that John was said to be illiterate. Unlike Matthew, John *was* an uneducated fisherman from Galilee. However, as with Peter, there's no reason why he couldn't have dictated his Gospel to a scribe. Ehrman himself acknowledges that this was a common practice in that time. He says, "Throughout most of antiquity, since most people could not write, there were local 'readers' and 'writers' who hired out their services."[223] It's for these reasons, among others, that New Testament scholar Raymond Brown concludes, "the combination of external and internal evidence associating the Fourth Gospel with John the son of Zebedee makes this the strongest hypothesis."[224]

## When Were the Gospels Written?

It's not uncommon to hear someone say that the Gospels were written hundreds of years after Jesus lived and that's why they're filled with myths and folklore about him. Neither of those claims are true.

First of all, the Gospels claim to report things that actually happened. They belong to the genre of historical biography, not historical fiction. Classifying the Gospels as biographies would have been laughed at a hundred years ago but classifying them this way makes the most sense based on what we know today. According to New Testament scholar

---

223 Ehrman, *Misquoting Jesus,* 38.
224 Raymond E. Brown, *The Gospel According to John,* vol. 1 (New York: Doubleday, 1966), xcviii.

Graham Stanton, "For a long time nearly all the standard books on the gospels stated confidently that the gospels are not biographies."[225] But now, he says, "I do not think it is . . . possible to deny that the Gospels are a subset of the broad literary genre of 'lives,' that is, biographies."[226]

Reza Aslan, a religious scholar who teaches at the University of California, Riverside, still presents the outdated view as if it were current. In *Zealot,* his New York Times bestseller about Jesus, Aslan says, "the gospels are not, nor were they ever meant to be, a historical documentation of Jesus' life."[227] This claim is simply false, and it's been known to be false for many decades now. John Kloppenborg is the chair of the department of religion at the University of Toronto who wrote an article on the Gospels for *The Oxford Encyclopedia of the Books of the Bible.* In his article, he pointed out that when the issue of the Gospels' genre was reexamined in the 1970s, taking into consideration the newer understandings of ancient literature, the conclusion was that they very closely matched the ancient category of biography.[228]

Saying that the Gospels are biographies doesn't mean to imply that they give us transcripts of everything Jesus said. Ancient biographies weren't like modern biographies. They didn't have audio or video recording equipment back then, nor were they interested in many aspects that are included in contemporary biographies. Brant Pitre points out that "ancient biographers were not as worried about *exactitude* as are modern biographers, who often want to provide the precise date, time, and place something happened."[229]

Instead, ancient biographers often organized their material thematically rather than chronologically and aimed at capturing the substance of what was said and done. Because of that, the portrait of Jesus in the

---

225 Graham Stanton, *The Gospels and Jesus,* 2nd ed. (Oxford, UK: Oxford University Press, 2002), 16.
226 Graham Stanton, foreword to *What Are the Gospels?,* 2nd ed., by Richard Burridge (Grand Rapids: Wm. B. Eerdmans, 2004), ix.
227 Reza Aslan, *Zealot: The Life and Times of Jesus of Nazareth* (New York: Random House, 2014), xxvi.
228 John S. Kloppenborg, "Gospels," in *The Oxford Encyclopedia of the Books of the Bible,* ed. Michael D. Coogan (New York: Oxford University Press, 2011), 342. Article: 334-349.
229 Pitre, *The Case for Jesus,* 74.

Gospels comes across more like a painting than a photograph. But that hardly validates the allegation that they're made up of myths and filled with folklore.

Beyond that, by ancient standards, the Gospels were written incredibly close to the time of the events which they claim to describe.[230] Even the most liberal approach to dating the Gospels has all of them being completed by the end of the first century, within seventy years of Jesus' life. Mark's Gospel is thought by the majority of scholars to have been written first, sometime after 70 AD. Matthew and Luke then incorporated some of the material from Mark's Gospel in their own Gospels, sometime in the 80s. And John's Gospel was written last, sometime in the mid to late 90s.

But the Gospels weren't published with dates attached to them, so why is Mark's Gospel thought to have been written after 70? There is one primary reason, and it's not a very convincing one. In Mark 13, Jesus warns that the Temple in Jerusalem will be destroyed in the future. The scene sounds very similar to what eventually happened to the Temple when it was destroyed by the Romans in 70 AD. Because some people doubt that Jesus could have predicted that event almost forty years before it happened, they say that Mark's Gospel must have been written after the Temple was destroyed and those words were then falsely attributed to Jesus.

But this way of reasoning is suspect. It's based on the assumption that Jesus couldn't have predicted the future destruction of the Temple. But why should that be assumed? It wouldn't have been difficult for Jesus to make such a prediction. All he had to do was look back at Israel's Scriptures, what Christians call the Old Testament.

When the Jewish leaders were acting unfaithfully, the prophets continually warned about the destruction that would come upon them. Eventually, destruction came in the form of a Babylonian invasion that laid siege to the Temple in Jerusalem. The event is described in 2 Kings 25:8-10. The Temple was burned and desecrated, and the walls around Jerusalem were torn down.

---

230 Paul Barnett, *Is the New Testament Reliable?*, 2nd ed. (Downers Grove: InterVarsity Press, 2003), 42.

As mentioned above, Jesus' ministry had a decidedly prophetic feel, and he continually spoke out against the corrupt Jewish religious leaders. It didn't take much imagination for him to connect his situation with the situation of the past, seeing Rome in the role of Babylon, and saying that a similar destruction would come their way.

Besides that, if Mark was writing (or someone was writing in Mark's name) after the destruction of the Temple in 70 AD, wouldn't it work to his advantage to add an editorial comment about it. It seems likely that he would have added something like, "We all saw that Jesus was right when the Romans destroyed the Temple a few years ago." But that's exactly what we don't have. Pitre points this out, saying, "the destruction of the Temple is never mentioned as a *past* event in any of the Gospels. If the Gospels were written after the destruction of the Temple in AD 70, then why don't the writers emphasize that Jesus's prophecy had been fulfilled? That would be the natural thing to do."[231]

It's reasonable to conclude that Mark's Gospel was written first, but it's unreasonable to conclude that it couldn't have been written before 70 AD. So, where does that leave us? What else do we know about the possible dates of the other Gospels?

We know that Luke's Gospel is a prequel to the book of Acts. Both documents are addressed to the same recipient, a person called Theophilus. Luke traveled with Paul and included many details about their journeys in the book of Acts. But the book of Acts ends in 62 AD with Paul under house arrest in Rome, still proclaiming the Good News about Jesus, and waiting for a meeting with Caesar. There's no mention of either the Temple's destruction in 70 or Paul's death, which most scholars place between 64 and 68. Because of that, Pitre suggests that "Luke stopped writing his story about Paul's life while Paul was in custody in Rome because *that's when the [book of Acts] was written* – around AD 62."[232]

Given the timeline of events, we can conclude that if the book of Acts is a sequel to Luke's Gospel, then Luke's Gospel must have been written before 62 AD. Not only that, but if Luke relied on

---
231 Pitre, *The Case for Jesus.*, 92.
232 Ibid., 99.

Mark's Gospel as a source in some way, which almost all scholars agree happened, then Mark's Gospel must have been written and put into circulation before Luke wrote his Gospel.

This chain of events means that Mark must have written his Gospel sometime in the mid-50s, only 25 years or so after the resurrection of Jesus. Given the way that oral culture actually worked, that's not enough time for legends and folklore to have taken over the stories about Jesus before they were written down.[233]

Also, the people who were alive when Jesus was around would have still been alive when the Gospels were written. There were eyewitnesses to the events described in the Gospels everywhere. They could have come forward and said that the Gospels were full of lies, but we have no record of that happening. What we *do* have is a record of the Christian movement spreading very quickly throughout the known world.[234] It was a movement of faith, hope, and love that was modeled on the one who had perfectly embodied those things.

## The Litmus Test

So, what should be the litmus test for the reliability of the Gospels? It isn't necessary, in my opinion, to begin with the belief that the Gospels are somehow divinely inspired. Christians *do* believe that, but it isn't where most people start. It's fair to start by reading the Gospels and asking whether their portrayal of Jesus is reasonably trustworthy. Does their portrayal of Jesus reflect what Jesus really said and did? Gregory Boyd is helpful on this point. He suggests, "we don't need to insist that [the Gospels'] presentation is historically accurate on every point or that it is entirely devoid of legendary accretion. We only need to accept that their testimony is *generally* reliable."[235]

People who start reading the Gospels with this question in mind might have doubts about a few of the stories that are reported; that's

---

[233] Kenneth Boa and Larry Moody, *I'm Glad You Asked: In-Depth Answers to Difficult Questions About Christianity* (Wheaton: Victor Books, 1982), 79.
[234] Rodney Stark, *The Rise of Christianity: A Sociologist Reconsiders History* (Princeton: Princeton University Press, 1996).
[235] Boyd, *Benefit of the Doubt*, 161.

okay. They might identify with the words of a man in Mark's Gospel who said to Jesus, "I do believe, but help me overcome my unbelief!" (Mark 9:24). Those doubts don't exclude people from taking a step of faith toward Jesus. Jesus invites those people to come to him. After all, the foundation of Christian faith is a person (Jesus) and an event (his resurrection), not a book. The person and the event were being talked about and bringing salvation to people's lives for decades before the books were ever written.[236]

## What We Covered in This Chapter

In this chapter, I addressed the question of the reliability of the Gospels. Before the first documents were written, the Good News about Jesus spread by word-of-mouth. It was an oral culture that emphasized memorization and prized the right-telling of stories. Despite claims that the Gospels circulated for almost a hundred years without titles or authors assigned to them, the historical record doesn't bear that out. The consensus throughout church history has been that Matthew wrote the Gospel of Matthew, Mark wrote the Gospel of Mark, Luke wrote the Gospel of Luke, and John wrote the Gospel of John. Those names wouldn't have gone very far in adding authority to the documents if they were falsely added later. In the final analysis, the Gospels in the New Testament provide us with at least a generally reliable account of what Jesus said and did. On that basis, we have every reason to trust them and put our faith in him.

In our next chapter, we'll conclude our conversation by looking at the differences between good faith and bad faith. Because if you're going to have faith, it might as well be good.

---

[236] Andy Stanley, *Irresistible: Reclaiming the New that Jesus Unleashed for the World* (Grand Rapids: Zondervan, 2018), 321.

# CHAPTER 8
## Where Do We Go from Here?

FOR CENTURIES, PEOPLE from all over the world and from all walks of life have been drawn to Jesus. They move from not knowing about him or not caring about him to believing in him and surrendering their lives to him. For some people, the move toward Jesus happens quickly. They hear the Good News about him and put their faith in him in what seems like an instant. For others, it happens slowly. They persist through a series of questions and conversations until they finally put the pieces together and trust Jesus to be the leader of their lives.

There isn't a right way or a wrong way to walk toward Jesus. The point is to start. In the New Testament, some people move slowly and other people move quickly. Peter is an example of someone who moved slowly. Through a series of successes and failures, and trials and errors, Peter eventually became one of the most influential leaders in the early church. Paul is an example of someone who moved quickly. He started out as a persecutor of the Christian movement. He believed they were lying about Jesus' resurrection and blaspheming God as a result. But all of that changed in an instant when he encountered the risen Jesus on the road to Damascus.

In our secular age, the idea of God has fallen on hard times. We've been told that God might be up there, out there, somewhere, but – even if he is – he isn't really interested or involved in what's going on right here, right now. It's up to us, then, to get on with our lives in whatever ways we see fit, without worrying about what a distant deity who probably doesn't exist might think about it. That was the message used for an atheist bus campaign in London from 2008 to 2009. During the campaign, which was sponsored by the British Humanist Association and Richard Dawkins, ads were posted on city buses that said, "There's probably no God. Now stop worrying and enjoy your life."

But we can't seem to outrun the feeling that we were made for more than that. We often catch glimpses of transcendence that go beyond what we thought was possible. If God isn't there and God doesn't care, then why can't we shake the sense that he *is* there, and he *does* care? Peter Berger suggests that in such moments, we're hearing "a rumor of angels."[237] And when we're honest, we can all hear the rumors.

We also recognize the shortcomings of a naturalistic storyline to explain the things that really matter in our lives. We long for meaning, hope, freedom, justice, and love. Humanism tells us that those things are worthless. But Jesus shows us that those things are worth dying for. Not only that, but Jesus says that we'll find those things which our hearts desire when we turn from sin and follow him. That's what it means to have faith.

So, in this final chapter, I want to share a few thoughts about faith because "*how* you believe and *what* you believe are two different things."[238] It's possible to believe the right things in the wrong ways. And if you're going to have faith in Jesus, you want it to be a good kind of faith.

## How to Have Good Faith

A good place to begin the conversation about good faith is by talking about what faith is and isn't. Bad understandings of faith can lead to bad expressions of faith, so it's important to clarify what faith actually means.

In his book, *Salvation by Allegiance Alone,* theologian Matthew Bates provides the clarification we need. He begins by listing four things that biblical faith is *not*. First, biblical faith doesn't mean that

---
[237] Peter L. Berger, *A Rumor of Angels: Modern Society and the Rediscovery of the Supernatural* (New York: Doubleday, 1969).
[238] Bell, *What We Talk About When We Talk About God,* 93.

we ignore relevant evidence and reason. Second, biblical faith doesn't mean that we make an illogical leap into the dark. Third, biblical faith doesn't mean that we feel a vague sense of optimism about the future. Fourth, biblical faith doesn't mean that we merely agree with certain claims about God.[239] It's unfortunate that many people think of faith in precisely these ways.

The New Testament was originally written in Greek, and the Greek word for faith is *pistis*. When we read the word "faith" in our English translations of the Bible, that's the word that was there in the Greek manuscripts. So, to understand what faith means, it's important to understand what *pistis* meant.

Bates does an extensive survey of how the word was used in the era of the New Testament and concludes that it means, "faithfulness, fidelity, or loyalty – that is, terms synonymous with the English word *allegiance*."[240] Therefore, biblical faith seems to be a settled conviction that Jesus is who he claimed to be, coupled with a focused intention to live how Jesus said to live. That's what it means to have faith in the biblical sense of the word.

Good faith is the outworking of *that* kind of faith. From there, good faith can be described as inquisitive, inclusive, active, and creative. Let's take a look at each of those in turn.

### *Good Faith is Inquisitive*

Good faith is inquisitive because it reminds us that we don't see the full picture or know the full story. It gives us a sense of honesty and humility about ourselves. It makes us curious about our place in the world. It frees us to wonder and ponder and ask questions as we seek to make sense of it all. It drives us into conversations about best practices and worthwhile objectives. It allows us to admit when we're wrong and not gloat when we're right. It doesn't settle for easy answers but pushes for clarity and nuance and truth. Bad faith is the opposite of that.

---

239 Matthew W. Bates, *Salvation by Allegiance Alone: Rethinking Faith, Works, and the Gospel of King Jesus* (Grand Rapids: Baker Academic, 2017), 15-25.
240 Ibid., 78.

## Good Faith is Inclusive

Good faith is inclusive because it refuses to let us shut conversations down or shut people out. It reminds us that all people are always welcome and worthy of love. It forces us to stay open. It moves us to value deep relationships and lasting community. It helps us offer dignity to others. It calls us to listen more than we talk. It allows us to lower our guard and hear what is truly being said. It opens us to empathy and offers us encouragement. It joins us with people who aren't like us to make the world better around us. Bad faith is the opposite of that.

## Good Faith is Active

Good faith is active because it recognizes the importance of integrity. It helps us push against hypocrisy by moving us to do what we say we'll do. It drives us to maintain alignment between our words and our actions. It reminds us that our lives represent our message, and what we do matters for ourselves and others. It inspires us to work in the present in light of the future. It calls us to open our eyes to the needs of people around us. It pushes us to do hard things and strive to make a difference, even when no one notices. Bad faith is the opposite of that.

## Good Faith is Creative

Good faith is creative because it resists the pull to move backward. It propels us forward to make new discoveries, find new connections, and blaze new trails. It pushes us to look at familiar things in fresh ways, to see what we haven't seen before. It leads us to consider alternatives. It opens us to experience surprises. It compels us to make something out of nothing. It calls us to bring beauty and goodness and blessing into the world. It helps us reject despair and embrace hope. It encourages us to be bold and live courageously. Bad faith is the opposite of that.

## The Choice is Yours

I believe that when Jesus invited people to enter the Kingdom of God by following him, he envisioned communities of people that would be known for these types of things. Later, when the Apostle Paul wanted to sum up what Christians should be known for, he settled on three words: faith, hope, and love. And he said that love is the most important (1 Corinthians 13:13). Where did Paul learn that? I'm convinced that he learned it from Jesus. When he thought about Jesus, he thought about love.

Elsewhere, he wrote, "I live in this earthly body by trusting in [Jesus], who loved me and gave himself for me" (Galatians 2:20). When Paul considered Christianity, he found that he couldn't run from the reality of love that he discovered in Jesus. It changed everything for him. But now the choice is yours. Where will you go from here?

## About the Author

TREVOR HAMAKER IS a Christian pastor and Bible teacher who helps people understand faith and apply it to their lives. He became a Christian as a senior in high school and has earned degrees in Business Management, Organizational Leadership. Religious Education, and Christian Theology. As a lifelong learner, he continues to seek honest answers to life's deepest questions.

Find out more and continue the conversation at trevorhamaker.blogspot.com.

Made in the USA
Coppell, TX
01 June 2021